L 3·45

DALES WAY

COMPANION

HILLSIDE GUIDES

LONG DISTANCE WALKS

1 • THE WESTMORLAND WAY

2 • THE FURNESS WAY

3 • THE CUMBERLAND WAY

7 • CLEVELAND WAY COMPANION

9 • THE NORTH BOWLAND TRAVERSE
(by David Johnson)

16 • DALES WAY COMPANION

CIRCULAR WALKS IN THE YORKSHIRE DALES

4 • WALKS IN WHARFEDALE

5 • WALKS IN NIDDERDALE

6 • WALKS IN THE CRAVEN DALES

8 • WALKS IN WENSLEYDALE

10 • WALKS IN THE WESTERN DALES

11 • WALKS IN SWALEDALE

12 • WALKS IN BRONTE COUNTRY (South Pennines)

CIRCULAR WALKS ON THE NORTH YORK MOORS

13 • WESTERN - Cleveland/Hambleton Hills

14 • SOUTHERN - Rosedale/Farndale/Bransdale

15 • NORTHERN - Eskdale and the Coast

DALES WAY COMPANION

by

Paul Hannon

HILLSIDE PUBLICATIONS
11 Nessfield Grove
Exley Head
Keighley
West Yorkshire
BD22 6NU

To the Ramblers
of the West Riding
'Dales Way pioneers'

Cover illustration: Barden Bridge
Page 1: Littondale, Birks Fell and upper Wharfedale from Conistone Pie

ISBN 1 870141 09 1

Printed in Great Britain by
Carnmor Print and Design
95/97 London Road
Preston
Lancashire
PR1 4BA

CONTENTS

The Old Bridge, Ilkley

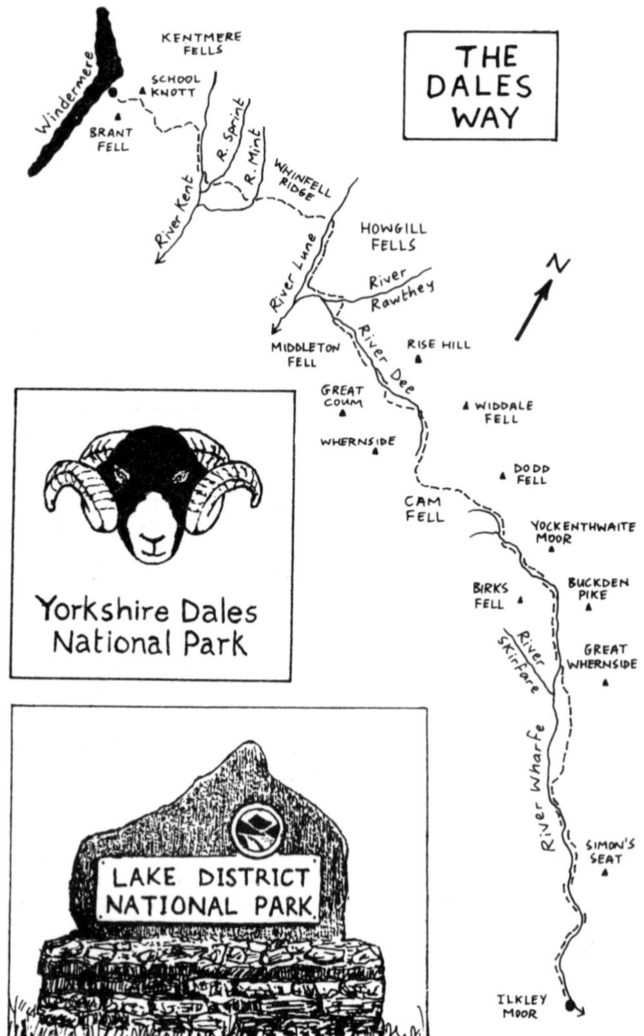
THE DALES WAY
KENTMERE FELLS
Windermere
SCHOOL KNOTT
BRANT FELL
R. Sprint
R. Mint
River Kent
WHINFELL RIDGE
HOWGILL FELLS
River Lune
River Rawthey
N
MIDDLETON FELL
River Dee
RISE HILL
GREAT COUM
WIDDALE FELL
WHERNSIDE
DODD FELL
CAM FELL
YOCKENTHWAITE MOOR
BIRKS FELL
BUCKDEN PIKE
River Skirfare
GREAT WHERNSIDE
River Wharfe
SIMON'S SEAT
ILKLEY MOOR
Yorkshire Dales National Park
LAKE DISTRICT NATIONAL PARK

INTRODUCTION

The Dales Way is an 84-mile long-distance path passing through the heart of the Yorkshire Dales and culminating in the Lake District. It is recognised by the Countryside Commission as a 'Recreational Path', and is a likely candidate for promotion to 'First Division' status as a 'National Trail', as our official long-distance routes may well become known.

The Way was the brainchild of the West Riding group of the Ramblers' Association, who could envisage the unquestionable appeal of a through route from the edge of the West Riding conurbations to the very shore of the country's largest lake. At the time of its inception in 1968, the Dales Way linked the counties of the West Riding of Yorkshire and Westmorland: both are now only history.

St. Wilfrids, Burnsall

The idea of following rivers through the Dales resulted in what is a well-defined route, namely the near-straight line through Wharfedale and Dentdale. The rivers Lune and Kent then chip in with a few miles during a crossing of undulating hills into the heart of lakeland.

An enterprising feature of those early plans was the addition of several 'link-paths', guiding footsteps from larger towns and cities to the start at Ilkley, and thereby further promoting the opportunities to walk out of the grime and into the green. A link with other long-distance routes was established with the arrival of the Ebor Way, a 70-mile walk between Ilkley and Helmsley, start of the Cleveland Way. Whilst on the subject, the Dales Way also encounters, further on its travels, the Pennine Way, the Ribble Way, and at the end, the author's Westmorland Way. Enough to be going on with?

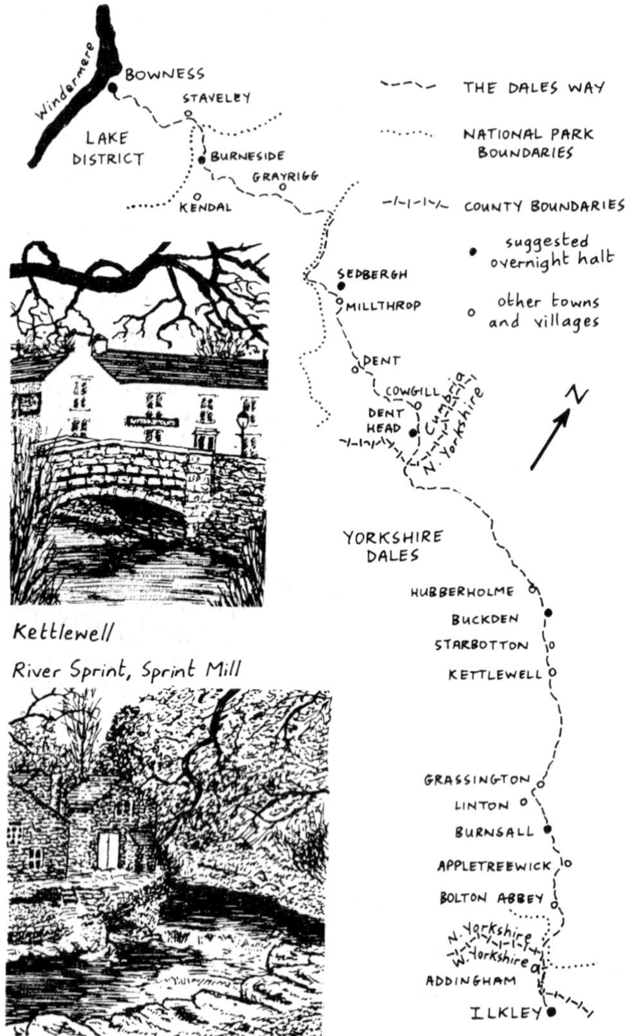

Kettlewell

River Sprint, Sprint Mill

The nature of the terrain of Dales Way country makes for a less demanding walk than many long-distance paths, and this has no doubt boosted its popularity, being a good choice for a first ever multi-day walk. Whilst it is largely a riverside route inside the Yorkshire Dales, the Way still grasps some opportunities to gain height along the valley sides of both Wharfedale and Dentdale, thus adding variety and more extensive views. Even down on the banks of the rivers one can usually enjoy distant vistas, thanks to the surround of high fells.

In the valleys many settlements are encountered, and all are delightfully individual places. They are most profuse in Wharfedale, which includes showpieces such as Kettlewell and Burnsall. Wonderful Dent, however, manages to equal anything before or after it. Highlights at the extremities of the walk are the romantic ruins of Bolton Priory and, only minutes off-route, the classic viewpoint of School Knott, which looks across Windermere to a magical line-up of lakeland fells.

Bridge End, Dent Head

Throughout the walk one is never far from some feature of architectural or historic interest, including a stone circle, a Roman road, a fourteenth century fortified manor house, a fifteenth century shooting lodge and a seventeenth century Quaker meeting house. Add to this a wealth of churches and bridges of all ages with, not surprisingly, the latter being most diverse. From packhorse bridge to suspension bridge, and concrete motorway bridge to Victorian viaduct, the Dales Way finds them all.

From Ilkley to Bowness the Dales Way - with very few reservations - takes the walker through scenery of the highest order, and though many will have already experienced the beauty of Wharfedale, far fewer will be aware of the delights awaiting beyond, so savour the Dee, Lune and Kent!

PLANNING THE WALK

The Dales Way runs from Ilkley to Bowness-on-Windermere, a distance of some 84 miles. It therefore fits ideally into a week, with an average distance of 14 miles over six days. The guide has been divided into that number of sections, each describing a day that will finish somewhere with suitable accommodation. Bed and breakfast establishments can be found throughout, with several youth hostels and more expensive hotels also on the route.

The only youth hostel at the end of a section is Dentdale, though Linton and Kettlewell can easily be incorporated by varying the lengths of the days. Kendal and Windermere hostels can also be made use of at the end of the final two days respectively. At Hubberholme and Beckermonds are two bunkbarns, with others only minutes off-route at Barden, and Catholes near Sedbergh.

A very useful feature of the Dales Way is the availability of public transport to and from the extremities of the walk. Both are by coincidence at the terminus of British Rail lines, Ilkley being served from Bradford and Leeds, while Windermere (1½ miles from Bowness) is served from Oxenholme on the Lancaster to Carlisle line. Both also have good bus services to the outside world.

The path itself is generally in good condition, with the first half through Wharfedale being the easiest to follow. Here most of the paths are already well trodden as a result of the valley's immense popularity and relative accessibility. The remote section beyond Sedbergh is, in fairly marked contrast, rarely visited, and consequently there is little evidence of previous walkers.

The Way passes through the territories of two National Park authorities, two county councils, and at the outset, a metropolitan council. Inevitably the condition of stiles and waymarking varies, but fortunately is at its best in the largest area, where the Dales Park's commitment to footpaths is highly commendable. Currently, the least signs of waymarking are on the most complicated stretch, between the two National Parks.

Even in areas where most rights-of-way are signposted, some omit any reference to the Dales Way, or even to the path's objective. The happy outcome (for the author at least!) is that a map/guide remains near-essential.

ORDNANCE SURVEY MAPS REQUIRED

These excellent maps complement the strip-maps in the guide by giving an overall picture of the countryside encountered, and showing the many off-route features which may be of use or interest.

1:50,000 Landranger

sheet 97 : Kendal + Morecambe
98 : Wensleydale + Upper Wharfedale
104 : Leeds, Bradford + Harrogate

Because of the detailed strip-maps in this guide, the above maps are more advantageous than the 1:25,000 (2½") maps, seven of which would be required to cover the walk:-

Outdoor Leisure 2 : Yorkshire Dales, Western area
7 : English Lakes, South East area
10 : Yorkshire Dales, Southern area
30 : Yorkshire Dales, Northern area
Pathfinder 617 : Sedbergh + Baugh Fell
662 : Bolton Abbey + Blubberhouses
671 : Keighley + Ilkley

EARLY CLOSING AND MARKET DAYS

	Early closing	*Market*
Ilkley	Wed.	Sat.
Grassington	Thur.	/
Sedbergh	Thur.	Wed.
Kendal	Thur.	Sat.
Bowness	Thur.	/

SOME RELEVANT READING

DALES WAY HANDBOOK - West Riding Ramblers' Association
lists buses, accommodation etc. – inexpensive and useful

THE DALES WAY – Colin Speakman (Dalesman) *good background*

DALES WAY ROUTE GUIDE - Arthur Gemmell + Colin Speakman (Stile)
route maps and return walks

ACROSS NORTHERN HILLS - Geoffrey Berry (Westmorland Gazette)
long distance walks, including a Dales Way chapter

SOME USEFUL FACILITIES

Below is a table of known facilities to be found on or near the Way. This is of necessity a general guide as many features are capable of changing rapidly. Known camping sites include Howgill, Appletreewick, Cowgill and Dent.

	YHA	other accom.	inn	bus service	railway	post office	other shop	WC	payphone
Ilkley		✓	✓	✓	✓	✓	✓	✓	✓
Addingham		✓	✓	✓		✓	✓	✓	✓
Bolton Bridge		✓	✓	✓					✓
Bolton Abbey		✓		✓		✓		✓	✓
Cavendish Pavilion							✓	✓	
Barden		✓		✓					✓
Howgill		✓		✓			✓		✓
Appletreewick		✓	✓	✓		✓			✓
Burnsall		✓	✓	✓		✓	✓	✓	✓
Hebden		✓	✓	✓		✓		✓	✓
Linton/Falls	✓	✓	✓	✓		✓		✓	✓
Grassington		✓	✓	✓		✓	✓	✓	✓
Conistone						✓			✓
Kettlewell	✓	✓	✓	✓		✓	✓	✓	✓
Starbotton		✓	✓	✓					✓
Buckden		✓	✓	✓		✓	✓	✓	✓
Hubberholme		✓	✓						
Yockenthwaite		✓							
Oughtershaw		✓							✓
Far Gearstones/B6255		✓		✓					
Dent Head	✓	✓							
Cowgill		✓	✓		✓				✓
Dent		✓	✓	✓		✓	✓	✓	✓
Millthrop				✓					
Sedbergh		✓	✓	✓		✓	✓	✓	✓
Lincoln's Inn Bridge				✓					
Lowgill		✓							✓
Grayrigg		✓		✓		✓			✓
Burton Hill/A6				✓					
Oakbank									✓
Kendal	✓	✓	✓	✓	✓	✓	✓	✓	✓
Burneside		✓	✓	✓	✓	✓	✓	✓	✓
Bowston		✓		✓					✓
Cowen Head									✓
Staveley		✓	✓	✓	✓	✓	✓	✓	✓
Bowness		✓	✓	✓		✓	✓	✓	✓

SOME USEFUL ADDRESSES

The Ramblers' Association
1/5 Wandsworth Road, London SW8 2XX
Tel. 01-582 6878

Youth Hostels Association
Trevelyan House, St. Albans, Herts. AL1 2DY
Tel. 0727-55215

Yorkshire Dales National Park
Office and Information Centre, Colvend, Hebden Rd, Grassington, Skipton, North Yorkshire BD23 5LB
Tel. Grassington (0756) 752748

Lake District National Park
Visitor Services, Brockhole, Windermere, Cumbria LA23 1LJ
Tel. Windermere (09662) 6601

Yorkshire and Humberside Tourist Board
312 Tadcaster Road, York YO2 2HF
Tel. York (0904) 707961

Cumbria Tourist Board
Ashleigh, Windermere, Cumbria LA23 2AQ
Tel. Windermere (09662) 4444

Ilkley Tourist Information, Station Road, Ilkley
Tel. Ilkley (0943) 602319

Sedbergh National Park Centre, Main Street, Sedbergh
Tel. Sedbergh (0587) 20125

Kendal Tourist Information, Town Hall, Highgate, Kendal
Tel. Kendal (0539) 25758

Bowness National Park Information, The Glebe, Bowness
Tel. Windermere (09662) 2895/5602

West Yorkshire Road Car Company
PO Box 24, East Parade, Harrogate, N. Yorks. HG1 5LS
Tel. Harrogate (0423) 66061

Ribble Motor Services
Blackhall Road, Kendal, Cumbria
Tel. Kendal (0539) 33221

Yorkshire Dales Society
152 Main Street, Addingham, Ilkley, West Yorkshire LS29 0LY

Friends of the Lake District
Kendal Road, Staveley, Kendal, Cumbria LA8 9LP

The above two organisations are not information services, but are deeply concerned with the well-being of the two areas, and provide an important 'watchdog' service in our much-abused Parks. Why not become a member?

THE ROUTE GUIDE

The bulk of this book is a detailed guide to the walk itself, extending from page 15 to page 81. It is divided into six daily sections, each of which has its own introduction: these can be located most easily by reference to the contents on page 5.

A continuous strip-map runs throughout the guide, accompanied by a narrative of the route on the same or facing page. The remainder of each page is then given over to notes and illustrations of the many places of interest along the way.

The maps are at the scale of 2½ inches to one mile, and the top of the page is always North.

Key to the map symbols

Route — clear — sketchy — no path

Route on public road — unenclosed — wall — Fence/hedge

Abbreviations g = gate s = stile c = cattle grid

Railway line

Buildings

Church

Cairns summit other

Limestone clints

Crags

Loose rock /scree

Marsh

Trees

river or beck — bridge — tarn or lake — waterfall

Miles from Ilkley

73

Map continuation (indicates page number)

39

SECTION 1

ILKLEY TO BURNSALL

13½ miles — 500 feet of ascent

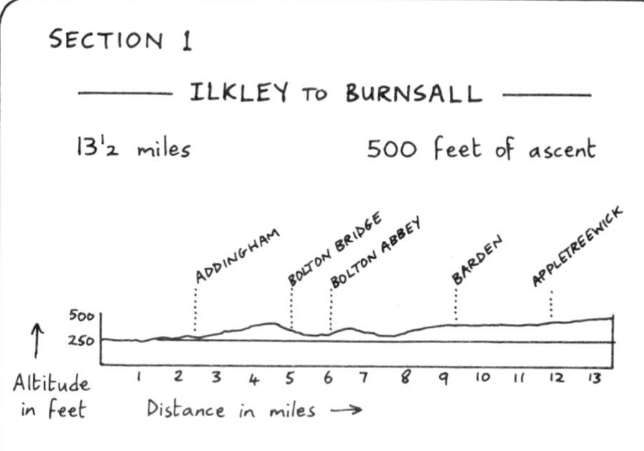

The opening day is reserved almost exclusively for the riverbank, far more so than any of the days ahead. As a result the walking is easy, and the surroundings happily still manage to vary enormously. Though Bolton Priory may be the highlight, Burnsall is a lovely spot to finish a day's walking. Youth hostellers may decide they want to press on the remaining easy miles to Linton.

Bolton Priory

Ilkley is the highest town on the Wharfe, and provides the perfect stepping stone between the industrial conurbations downstream and the joys of the Yorkshire Dales immediately upstream. Travelling up the Wharfe, it is only on reaching Ilkley that the enclosing hills first show their more serious intentions, and none more so than the world-famous Ilkley Moor rising steeply to the south of the town with which it is synonymous. Its breezy heather heights are in fact only a modest tract of the extensive, all-embracing Rombalds Moor, which boasts a wealth of antiquity in stone, with circles, cairns and carvings. Also above the town are the Cow and Calf rocks, the Tarn, and Hebers Gill, all being popular local haunts.

Although Ilkley's origins are far earlier, it is perhaps best known as the Roman's 'Olicana', and for some superb Anglian crosses, now inside the parish church. Alongside the church is the very attractive Manor House, now serving as a museum. Ilkley's real growth came with the railway, and its humble pretentions to being a spa resort: to this day it has attracted wealth, in the form of businessmen seeking a haven from city workplaces, and people set for relaxing retirement amidst invigorating air.

19
This is a charming corner, with the Way making use of two delightful approaches to the church.
Addingham
2
Castleberg Scar
Low Mill Village
Here North Yorkshire makes a brief foray across the river
ADDINGHAM
River Wharfe
A holiday complex may devastate this green pasture
ILKLEY

The bustling village of Addingham straddles the Ilkley - Skipton road where it begins its climb over into Airedale. The coming of the industrial revolution transformed this long established street-village only after a good deal of Luddite opposition, but this highest point on the Wharfe to find mills in any numbers, now finds them replaced by housing schemes or at best modern industry. A further transformation should be occuring here when a long-awaited by-pass eventually appears. Away from the main street and its five scattered hostelries, the parish church of St. Peter stands in tranquillity above the Wharfe.

ILKLEY to ADDINGHAM

The Route

The Dales Way officially begins at the Old Bridge over the Wharfe, which is best gained by turning down New Brook Street from the traffic lights by the parish church. Before the modern road bridge descend to accompany the river upstream to the Old Bridge.

Without crossing this shapely structure continue upstream on a surfaced path which soon joins the access road to Ilkley's tennis club. Bear round to the buildings and then break off to a gate on the left. A field-path now heads off through half a dozen pastures, each of which is linked by kissing-gates. The Wharfe is regained, albeit briefly, until it nudges us up onto a quiet back road parallel with the main Ilkley-Addingham highway.

Head along the road and at the first chance fork right on the access road to Low Mill Village. Forge on between the houses and onto an enclosed way which becomes another back road now on the edge of Addingham. When level with the parish church take the obvious path to it, then turn left along another path which crosses a tiny bridge to emerge between houses onto North Street.

The Wharfe's name originates from the Celtic meaning 'swift water', and this lovely river races almost 30 miles through the National Park before a more sedate journey to meet the Ouse near Selby.

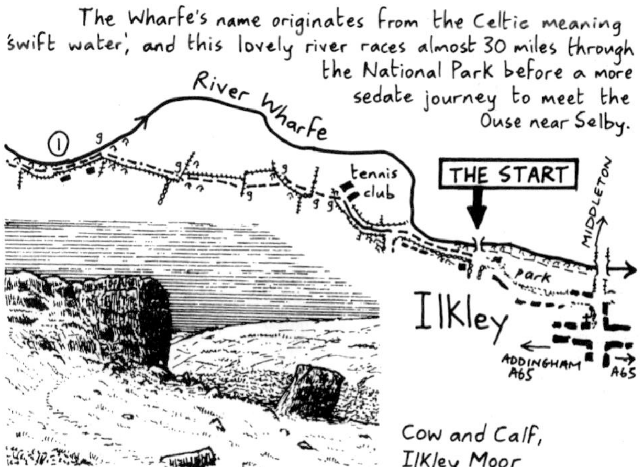

Cow and Calf, Ilkley Moor

The Route

Unless wishing to enter the village centre, turn right along North Street (becoming Bark Lane) and opt for a footpath branching right, down to the river. Without crossing the footbridge turn upstream, keeping close to the Wharfe at an early fork. High Mill soon deflects us away from the river: enter the caravan park straight ahead, to take a gate on the right part-way through to rejoin the Wharfe.

The riverbank now leads unfailingly up the dale, though at a steep bank of trees we are pointlessly forced up onto the near-parallel road for literally a couple of yards only. After several more pastures we must climb back to the road again, a stile leading into the trees where we skirt the garden of a house to find a stile onto the road.

The Way now follows the often busy B6160 road almost to Bolton Bridge, a short path taking to the river again for a direct route to the bridge. A good alternative path avoids most of the rather dangerous road-walk, and is described opposite.

Bolton Bridge

ADDINGHAM to BOLTON BRIDGE

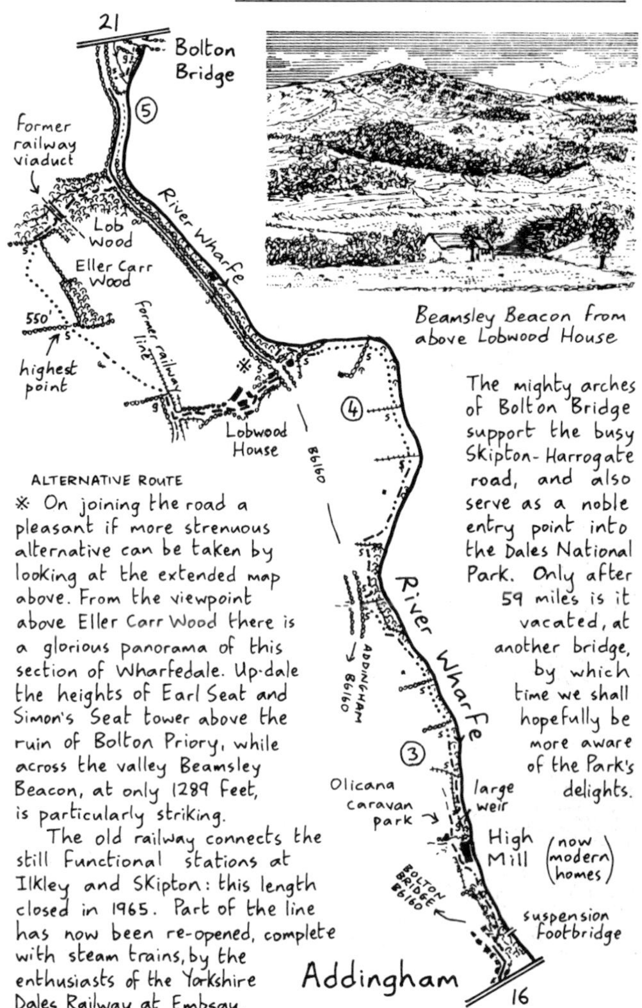

Beamsley Beacon from above Lobwood House

The mighty arches of Bolton Bridge support the busy Skipton-Harrogate road, and also serve as a noble entry point into the Dales National Park. Only after 59 miles is it vacated, at another bridge, by which time we shall hopefully be more aware of the Park's delights.

ALTERNATIVE ROUTE

※ On joining the road a pleasant if more strenuous alternative can be taken by looking at the extended map above. From the viewpoint above Eller Carr Wood there is a glorious panorama of this section of Wharfedale. Up-dale the heights of Earl Seat and Simon's Seat tower above the ruin of Bolton Priory, while across the valley Beamsley Beacon, at only 1289 feet, is particularly striking.

The old railway connects the still functional stations at Ilkley and Skipton: this length closed in 1965. Part of the line has now been re-opened, complete with steam trains, by the enthusiasts of the Yorkshire Dales Railway at Embsay.

The Route

At Bolton Bridge cross the road with care and from a stile continue up the Wharfe's western bank, an extensive riverside pasture guiding us peacefully towards the increasingly imposing ruin of Bolton Priory. After a suitable exploration cross the wooden footbridge for a first taste of the Wharfe's eastern bank, and after short-cutting a loop of the river continue upstream in the trees.

A higher, parallel path enters the trees earlier, and after a stile a path forks uphill to join it. A little further on a narrow road is joined just prior to it fording Pickles Beck, where a footbridge a few yards above caters for those not wishing to clean their boots. On the other side a stile returns us to the river to arrive at the Cavendish Pavilion bridge. On crossing it turn right to the Nature Trail shop, where an entry fee is usually payable for access into the private woods ahead: a wide path then commences this fine woodland walk.

Tithe Barn, Bolton Abbey

BOLTON BRIDGE to STRID WOOD

Bolton Abbey is, strictly, the name of the tiny village whose showpiece is more correctly the Priory. The imposing ruin is a magnet for close-at-hand West Yorkshire visitors, with the river hereabouts being an attraction in its own right. The priory dates from 1154 and was built by Augustinian canons who moved here from nearby Embsay. At the dissolution the nave was spared, and remains to this day the parish church.

There is much else of interest in the vicinity including adjacent Bolton Hall dating from the 17th century; and up by the post office a large and splendid example of a tithe barn. Also here is the 'Hole in the Wall', providing a classic framed view of the priory's surroundings.

At Bolton Bridge the large hotel bears the arms of the Duke of Devonshire, which comes as no surprise as almost everything hereabouts still belongs to that estate.

From Bolton Bridge to Barden Bridge, almost all of the route is on the estate's permissive paths.

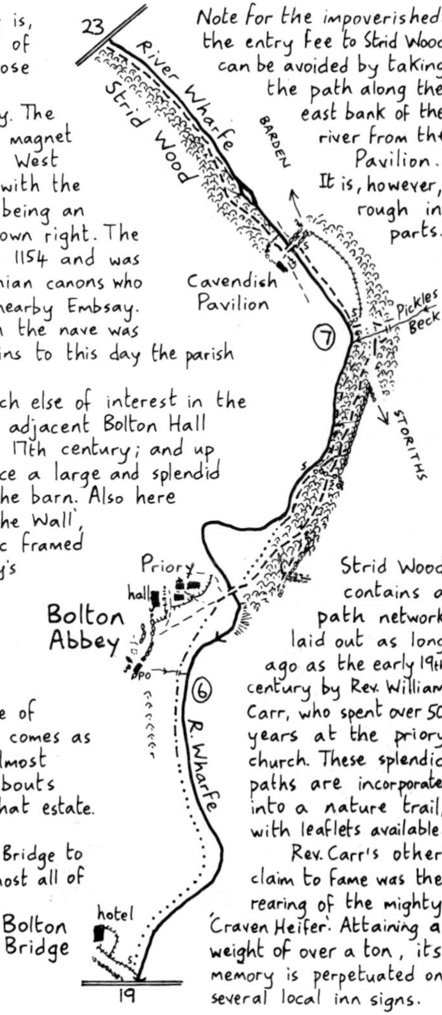

Note for the impoverished: the entry fee to Strid Wood can be avoided by taking the path along the east bank of the river from the Pavilion. It is, however, rough in parts.

Strid Wood contains a path network laid out as long ago as the early 19th century by Rev. William Carr, who spent over 50 years at the priory church. These splendid paths are incorporated into a nature trail, with leaflets available.

Rev. Carr's other claim to fame was the rearing of the mighty 'Craven Heifer'. Attaining a weight of over a ton, its memory is perpetuated on several local inn signs.

The Route

Remain on the main riverside path (green Nature Trail markers) for easy walking to The Strid, a modest detour being required to view it. From here the initially higher path (yellow markers) is the most used, merging above the High Strid to soon arrive at a stile out of the woods. Within a couple of minutes a sturdy aqueduct is crossed to resume the journey on the opposite bank, with Barden Bridge, in turn, soon being reached.

Without crossing it head straight along the road for a short distance, then turn through the trees to a stile to return to the riverbank. The Wharfe is hugged comprehensively now until our path is forced up onto the road at Howgill by the inflowing Fir Beck.

Barden Tower

A very worthwhile detour is provided by a short climb from Barden Bridge to Barden Tower, which is an imposing ruin. Largely used as a hunting lodge by the powerful Cliffords of Skipton Castle, it also boasted two famous residents from that family. Henry, the 'Shepherd' Lord, came in 1485, being raised in the Cumbrian fells until the Wars of the Roses ended. Until his death in 1523 he preferred Barden's peace and the company of the canons of Bolton to Skipton's splendour. He also had the adjacent chapel built.

The redoubtable Lady Anne had the Tower restored in 1659 and spent much of her final years here, a stone plaque affixed to an outside wall surviving to confirm her work. In 1676 she died, last of the Cliffords, and the long process of decay began.

STRID WOOD to HOWGILL

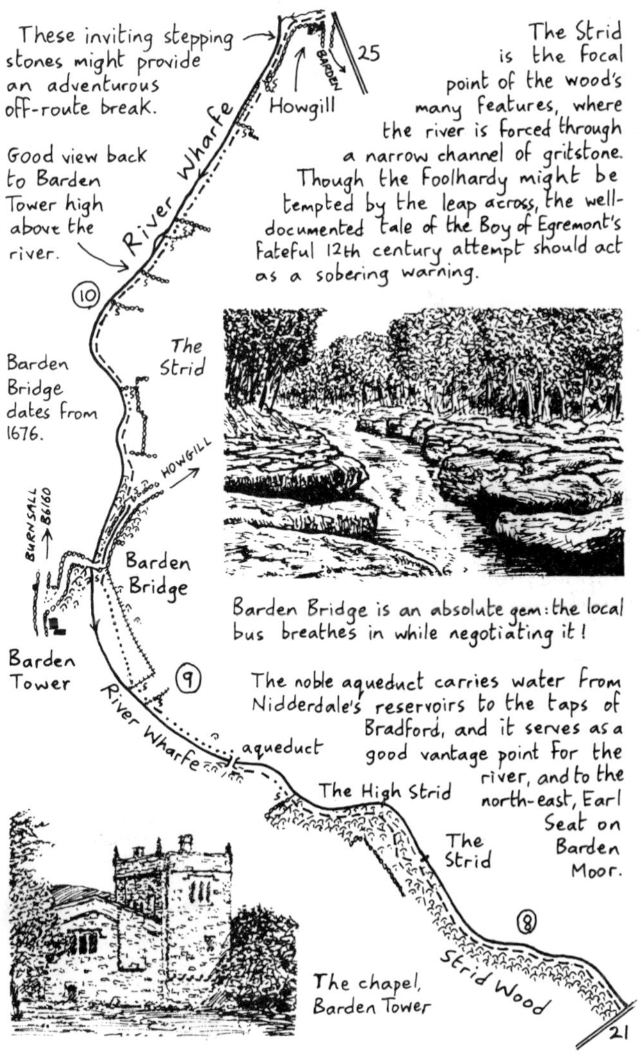

The Strid is the focal point of the wood's many features, where the river is forced through a narrow channel of gritstone. Though the foolhardy might be tempted by the leap across, the well-documented tale of the Boy of Egremont's fateful 12th century attempt should act as a sobering warning.

Barden Bridge is an absolute gem: the local bus breathes in while negotiating it!

The noble aqueduct carries water from Nidderdale's reservoirs to the taps of Bradford, and it serves as a good vantage point for the river, and to the north-east, Earl Seat on Barden Moor.

The chapel, Barden Tower

The Route

From the road bridge over Fir Beck we return immediately to the river through a pasture locked between water and woods. The Wharfe is now shadowed almost all the way to Burnsall, passing below Appletreewick on the way (see note regarding detour to it).

The only break from the river occurs when the farmstead of Woodhouse intervenes - here we by-pass a loop of the Wharfe by turning right through the yard, straight on to a footbridge and across a field back to the river. When Burnsall Bridge appears the final field is crossed directly to a stile at the start of the bridge, which is then crossed itself to enter the village.

Woodhouse is a seventeenth century manor house alongside the lively Barben Beck.

Access to Appletreewick is via the enclosed path beyond Low Hall, but many walkers make use of an earlier track ※ which rises directly to the New Inn. Though not a right-of-way, the farmer provides riverside access in the season, and a few coppers in the top gatepost should maintain this happy situation.

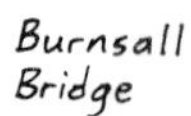

Burnsall Bridge

HOWGILL to BURNSALL

Appletreewick has several claims to fame, although many visitors may best remember its delightful name. Here are three halls and two inns in amongst a wonderful assortment of cottages. All stand by the narrow road wandering through the village, from High Hall at the top - note the tiny church nearby - to Low Hall at the very bottom. Probably the oldest however is the interestingly named Mock Beggar Hall, a fine little structure once known as Monk's Hall.

Of the two hostelries one takes its name from the family of William Craven, a Dick Whittington character who found his fortune in London, becoming Lord Mayor in 1611. Not forgetting his beginnings he became a worthy local benefactor, having Burnsall's grammar school and a number of bridges in the district built. Its fellow inn, meanwhile, achieved national fame in recent years thanks to the enterprising 'no-smoking' policy of a previous landlord. Today it is equally enterprising in its extensive range of fascinating beers from abroad.

Simon's Seat from the Wharfe at Appletreewick

The river scenery in the vicinity of Howgill is of a particularly high order. On rejoining the river, note the simple memorial plate set into a rock - and read it carefully!

Howgill itself is a scattered hamlet in the shadow of Simon's Seat. It is a gateway to Skyreholme valley with its famous limestone gorge of Trollers Gill, and fine house and gardens of Parceval Hall. Howgill boasts tea rooms, camping site and adjacent shop, lonely Methodist chapel and lovely bluebell wood.

R. Wharfe
APPLETREEWICK
11
23
Howgill

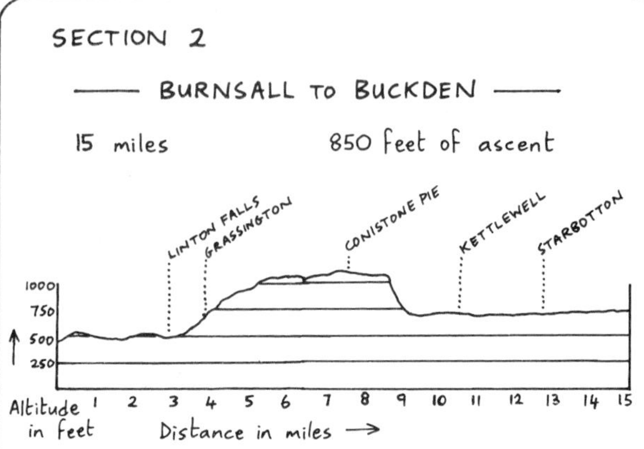

This glorious expedition through the heart of Wharfedale is composed of three distinct sections. Classic riverside paths connect famous huddled villages, but form only the outers of a sandwich whose filling is a meaty one, an unforgettable upland traverse between limestone ledges. If the weather is kind then extensive views will be enjoyed across the rolling Dales, from the underfoot comfort of luxuriant green turf.

Fox and Hounds, Starbotton

BURNSALL to LOUP SCAR

The Route

From Burnsall Bridge the river is rejoined immediately by a wide path now on its western bank. This heavily-walked section soon escapes from the village and runs happily upstream to rise to a gate above the gorge of Loup Scar.

Below: Loup Scar

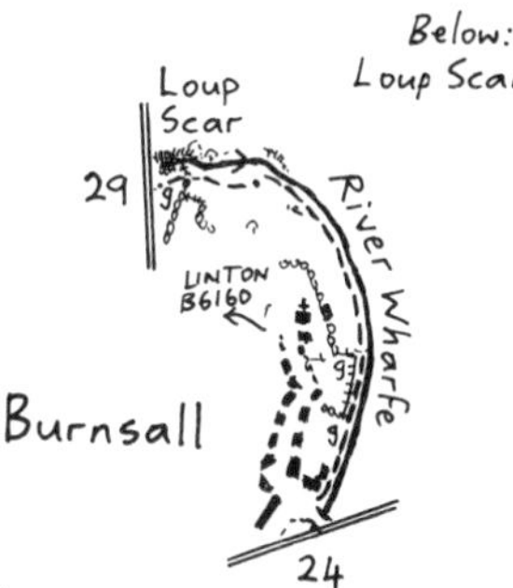

At Loup Scar the Wharfe flows through an impressive limestone fault. This is a place to linger, as sunny summer weekends testify.

Burnsall's setting is one of near-perfection, with bridge, green - and maypole - church, inn and cottages fusing into an unforgettable Wharfedale scene. St. Wilfrid's church is just outside the village centre, but worth a short walk up the road past the post office. It dates largely from the fifteenth century and has an inscribed Norman font - note also the functional lych-gate. Alongside is the lovely village school, founded in 1602 by William Craven as one of the earliest grammar schools.

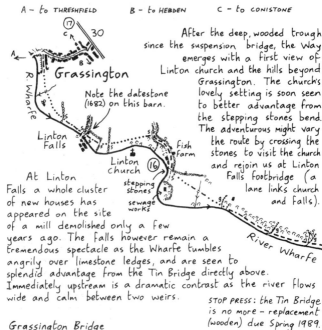

A – to THRESHFIELD B – to HEBDEN C – to CONISTONE

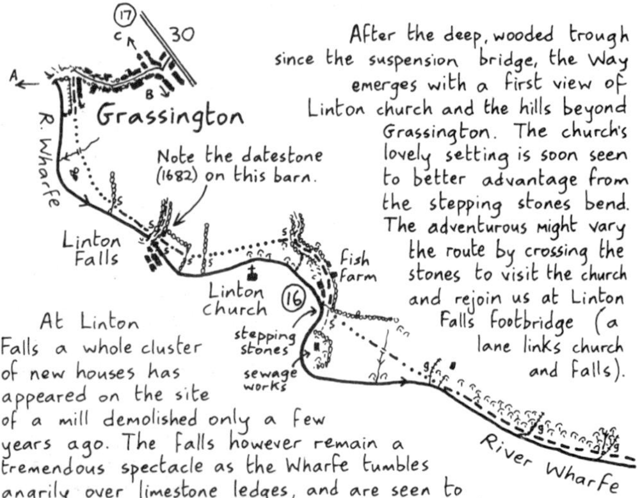

17
30
Grassington
R. Wharfe
Note the datestone (1682) on this barn.
Linton Falls
Linton Church
16
fish farm
stepping stones
sewage works
River Wharfe

After the deep, wooded trough since the suspension bridge, the Way emerges with a first view of Linton church and the hills beyond Grassington. The church's lovely setting is soon seen to better advantage from the stepping stones bend. The adventurous might vary the route by crossing the stones to visit the church and rejoin us at Linton Falls footbridge (a lane links church and falls).

At Linton Falls a whole cluster of new houses has appeared on the site of a mill demolished only a few years ago. The falls however remain a tremendous spectacle as the Wharfe tumbles angrily over limestone ledges, and are seen to splendid advantage from the Tin Bridge directly above. Immediately upstream is a dramatic contrast as the river flows wide and calm between two weirs.

STOP PRESS: the Tin Bridge is no more – replacement (wooden) due Spring 1989.

Grassington Bridge

LOUP SCAR to GRASSINGTON

The Route

From the gate above Loup Scar the path drops down to run through some lovely wooded environs to the suspension footbridge below Hebden village. On crossing it a very straightforward walk ensues through a reach that is deeply enclosed. On emerging, a loop in the Wharfe is avoided by striking across a large pasture (footbridge midway) to the right of a tree-masked sewage works.

On gaining the access road to the works take a stile on the right and accompany it past a fish farm and away from the river. As the track climbs through a bend take a stile on the left to regain the Wharfe's company opposite Linton church. Through several fields we arrive at the Tin Bridge at Linton Falls.

Without crossing the bridge continue by the river, rising a little away from it after an intervening wall, and continuing on to meet an enclosed path beneath a terrace of houses. This empties onto the main road above Grassington Bridge. The road can now be followed up to the right to the centre of Grassington, the central square being up to the left when the main road bends sharply right.

15
River Wharfe
HEBDEN
BURNSALL
suspension footbridge
Loup Scar
27
14

The suspension bridge spans a wide, calm stretch of the river, and bears a 1985 centenary plaque. Immediately downstream are some defunct stepping stones.

Approaching the suspension bridge there is a glimpse up to the colourful slopes and scars of Hebden Gill.

Also attainable by ancient stepping stones from Hebden...

St. Michael and All Angels, Linton

Grassington is the undisputed 'capital' of upper Wharfedale, a thriving community with a wide range of services. The splendid cobbled square is the focal point, but really is only the shop window: hidden away is much of interest. Historically, Grassington boasted an 18th century theatre and a lead mining industry of which its nearby moor displays much evidence. Buildings of interest include the Old Hall and the former Town Hall-cum-Institute. Here also is a folk museum, the National Park offices and a purpose built (1988) National Park Centre alongside.

The Route

From Grassington's square head up the main street past the Devonshire Arms to a crossroads, and there turn left along Chapel Street. When it eventually turns sharply left, leave it for the farmyard on the right, keeping right of the main buildings and just skirting them to arrive at a gate after the last building.

Leave the gate by following the right-hand wall away, and at the end take the middle one of three gates. Bear left across the next field to a painfully narrow gap-stile at the far end. In the next pasture curve round to the left to a stile in the far wall, behind which another stile admits onto the large expanse of Lea Green.

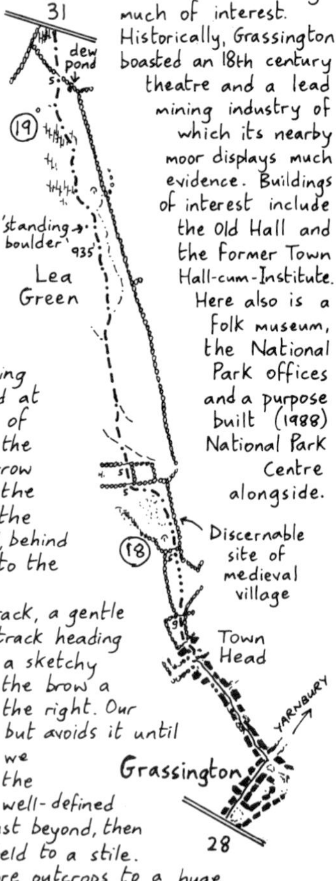

After crossing a wider track, a gentle rise leads up to join another track heading our way. A little further on a sketchy left fork is ignored, and at the brow a near-parallel wall is seen to the right. Our sketchy path remains near it but avoids it until beyond a limestone pavement we descend to a stile just before the corner. Head away to skirt a well-defined area of outcrops to a gate just beyond, then rise across the bottom of a field to a stile.

Maintain the rise past more outcrops to a huge kiln and a stile beyond. Level pastures then precede a pull to the head of Conistone Dib. Avoid the stile and take the briefly enclosed way to its right to emerge onto a wide track. Cross over and pass below a scar to a stile below the knoll of Conistone Pie.

GRASSINGTON to CONISTONE PIE

Lea Green is the site of an ancient British settlement, the field system being best appreciated by aerial view (balloon flights operate from Grassington).

Conistone Pie is an inviting little eminence visible from numerous parts of the upper dale. From a distance it resembles a man-made tower, though closer inspection soon reveals its natural limestone architecture.

Crowned by a fine cairn, this sentinel boasts a marvellous panorama across the deep trough of Wharfedale. Most impressive is the dale-head beneath 2000-foot fells, although eyes may first be drawn to the twin-like fork of Littondale striking away from beneath us. The confluence of its river, the Skirfare, with the Wharfe can be picked out from the path, while close by is the famous overhang of Kilnsey Crag.

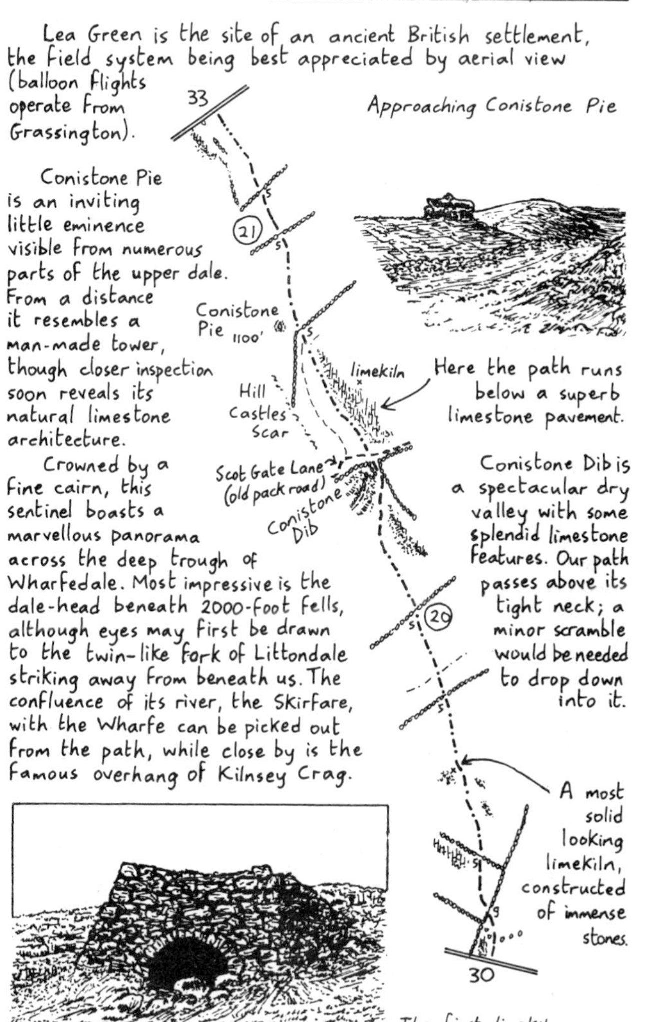

Approaching Conistone Pie

Here the path runs below a superb limestone pavement.

Conistone Dib is a spectacular dry valley with some splendid limestone features. Our path passes above its tight neck; a minor scramble would be needed to drop down into it.

A most solid looking limekiln, constructed of immense stones.

The first limekiln

The Route

Beyond Conistone Pie the path heads clearly away, soon running a very level course over stiles in intervening walls. Though the path fades, the route remains in little doubt below limestone outcrops. When the attendant scar expires go straight to a stile by a gate into the corner of a plantation. A wide track now descends the hillside, passing near Scargill House on the right before turning left to emerge onto a back road from Conistone to Kettlewell.

Turn right along this narrow road past the drive to Scargill House, and after a couple of kinks in it take a gate on the right at a footpath sign. Head away to a gateway then turn through it to a gate in the next wall, here commencing a fascinating course taking in about one dozen fields within half a mile.

Though not visible on the ground, the Way follows a near-straight wall, twice switching to its opposite side before emerging at the head of a narrow green lane on the edge of Kettlewell. Turn down it to a T-junction and then right to emerge onto a back lane. Now go left, passing the Kings Head and then right at the maypole to reach the main road through the village.

Upper Wharfedale from above Highgate Leys Lane, with Birks Fell (left), Yockenthwaite Moor and the slopes of Buckden Pike

CONISTONE PIE to KETTLEWELL

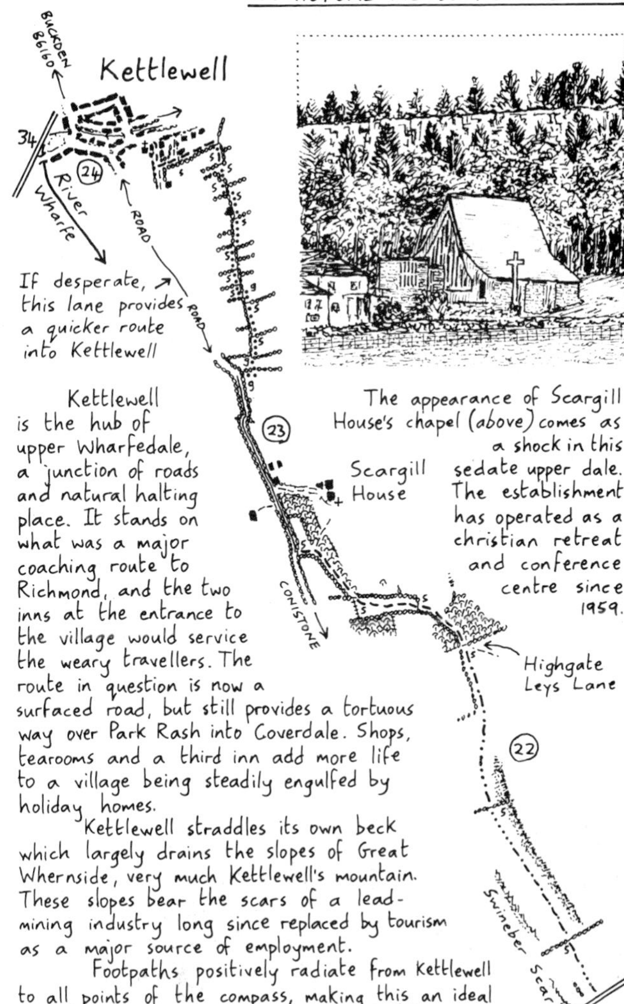

Kettlewell is the hub of upper Wharfedale, a junction of roads and natural halting place. It stands on what was a major coaching route to Richmond, and the two inns at the entrance to the village would service the weary travellers. The route in question is now a surfaced road, but still provides a tortuous way over Park Rash into Coverdale. Shops, tearooms and a third inn add more life to a village being steadily engulfed by holiday homes.

Kettlewell straddles its own beck which largely drains the slopes of Great Whernside, very much Kettlewell's mountain. These slopes bear the scars of a lead-mining industry long since replaced by tourism as a major source of employment.

Footpaths positively radiate from Kettlewell to all points of the compass, making this an ideal base for a week's holiday without need of transport.

The appearance of Scargill House's chapel (above) comes as a shock in this sedate upper dale. The establishment has operated as a christian retreat and conference centre since 1959.

The Route

Leave Kettlewell by turning left along the main road out of the village over the Wharfe, then at once take a gate on the right. A few yards along a track, a path forks down to the river and heads upstream, soon to be deflected a little above the river and on – sometimes enclosed by walls – through many pastures. The Wharfe, never more than a fields-length away, eventually comes closer again to play a game of hide-and-seek. Though occasionally sketchy underfoot, the Way remains fairly obvious to soon arrive at the Starbotton footbridge.

From the bridge our route remains on the western bank, though the Wharfe soon breaks away again. The path heads straight on by the left-hand wall, and on occasions is fully enclosed before the river is encountered again. Here the briefly sketchy path rises from a gate in an intervening fence to join a wide track. Shortly after passing a barn the Wharfe breaks away again, but this time we join it by dropping down to a gate in a wall. From here the river's meandering course is hugged for the short journey to Buckden Bridge.

From Kettlewell to Buckden note the symmetry of this glacier-made U-shaped valley.

The village of Starbotton is situated just off-route across the Wharfe, midway between its larger and better known neighbours, Kettlewell and Buckden. Though the valley road passes through, few visitors pause here: the usual reason for halting is the attractive whitewashed inn. Off the main road are some lovely corners, with an old Quaker burial ground hidden away.

Starbotton nestles beneath the slopes of Buckden Pike, and like its neighbours stands above the river on its own swift-flowing beck. This, Cam Gill Beck, was swollen in 1686 by a deluge which caused disastrous flooding.

KETTLEWELL to BUCKDEN

In medieval times Buckden was the headquarters of a vast hunting forest, the name of the inn recalling its importance.

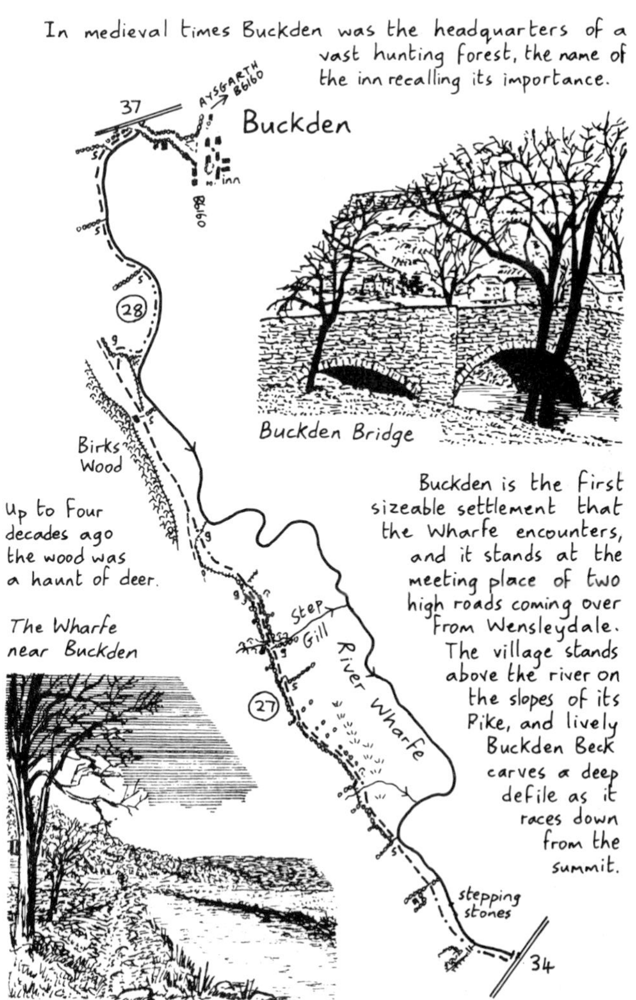

Buckden Bridge

The Wharfe near Buckden

Up to four decades ago the wood was a haunt of deer.

Buckden is the first sizeable settlement that the Wharfe encounters, and it stands at the meeting place of two high roads coming over from Wensleydale. The village stands above the river on the slopes of its Pike, and lively Buckden Beck carves a deep defile as it races down from the summit.

SECTION 3

BUCKDEN TO DENT HEAD

16½ miles — 1500 feet of ascent

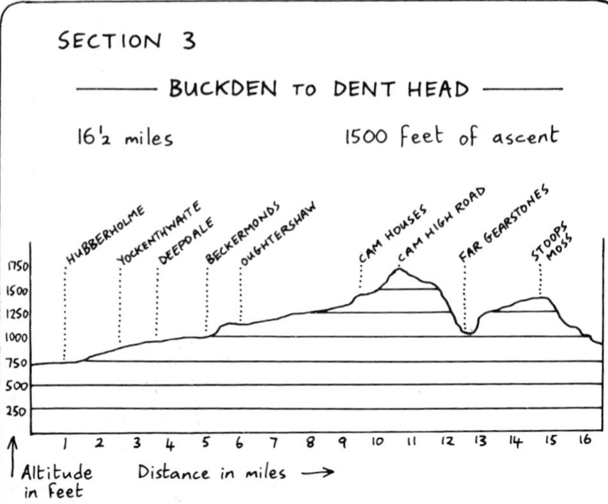

During this section the Way attains its highest point at 1710 feet on Cam Fell. Naturally enough this day marks the linking of the walk's two major valleys, though a brief flirtation with the headwaters of the Ribble interrupts the Wharfe-Dee crossing. Similar to yesterday the upland section (this time bleaker) divides riverside walks: in beautiful Langstrothdale we positively hug the vibrant Wharfe, while the infant Dee is equally shadowed by a narrow and fairly quiet road.

George Inn, Hubberholme

BUCKDEN to HUBBERHOLME

Though barely even a hamlet, Hubberholme boasts two famous buildings and a shapely bridge which connects them. The church of St. Michael is a gem, with its tower showing Norman traces. Its best feature is a 500-year old oak rood loft, one of only two remaining in Yorkshire, while some pews bear the famous trademark of 'Mousey' Thompson. Outside, meanwhile, the sparkling Wharfe runs almost past its very door.

Across the river is the whitewashed and homely George Inn in an idyllic setting. Formerly housing the vicar, its flagged floors continued to be the scene of the New Year 'land-letting', when the proceeds from a poor pasture go to the needy parishioners.

St. Michael's Hubberholme

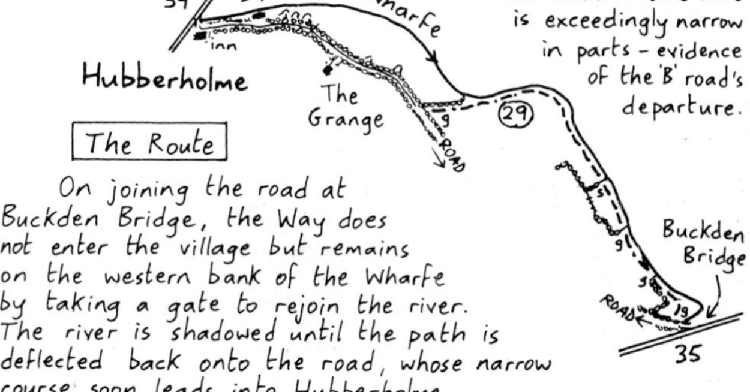

The Hubberholme lane is exceedingly narrow in parts - evidence of the 'B' road's departure.

The Route

On joining the road at Buckden Bridge, the Way does not enter the village but remains on the western bank of the Wharfe by taking a gate to rejoin the river. The river is shadowed until the path is deflected back onto the road, whose narrow course soon leads into Hubberholme.

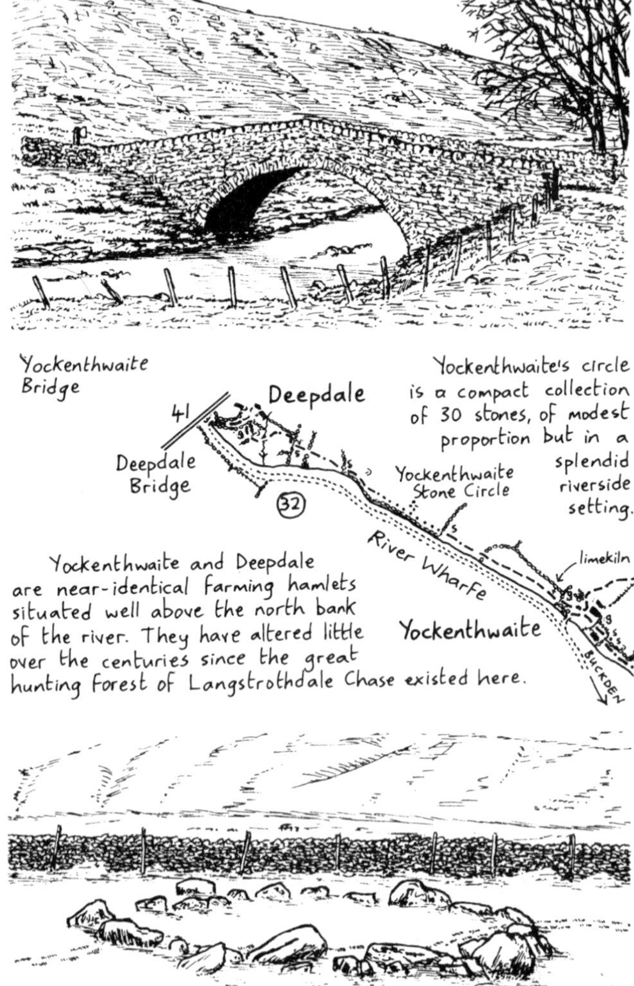

Yockenthwaite Bridge

Yockenthwaite's circle is a compact collection of 30 stones, of modest proportion but in a splendid riverside setting.

Yockenthwaite and Deepdale are near-identical farming hamlets situated well above the north bank of the river. They have altered little over the centuries since the great hunting forest of Langstrothdale Chase existed here.

Yockenthwaite Stone Circle

HUBBERHOLME to DEEPDALE

The Route

At Hubberholme cross the bridge and take a gate to the right of the church. Beyond the churchyard wall leave the wide access track climbing the hill, and cross the pasture to regain the river. The next settlement up-dale is Yockenthwaite, and the Way remains clear throughout as it never strays more than a few yards from the Wharfe.

At Yockenthwaite pass to the right of the first of the buildings, then head straight on, avoiding temptation to descend to the shapely bridge. Passing above a diminutive wooded enclosure at a gate, we are back in the company of the river. After a couple of pastures the track fades as it passes Yockenthwaite's stone circle, but from a stile beyond it a faint path materialises to rise away from the Wharfe through a gap to another stile.

Cross the field-top to a footbridge at the far side, then go on through a gap to a gate to join the access road up to Deepdale. Turn down it to reach the road and cross straight over the uninspiring bridge.

A glance at the 1:50,000 Ordnance map will reveal countless alternatives to the designated routes of long-distance walks, but the Dales Way probably has more choice than most. One such option is included on the extended map below, being a higher-level route between Hubberholme and Yockenthwaite.

Only a brief climb to Scar House is required before extensive views over the upper dale can then be enjoyed. Immediately across the valley is Birks Fell, 2001'.

Scar House 1100' ← an early Quaker meeting place

31

30

River Wharfe

HAWES

37

Hubberholme

Above Hubberholme the path cleverly avoids whichever bank the road occupies.

Oughtershaw is the first - or in our case, last - settlement of any size in Wharfedale. Although more than 1100 feet up its setting is far from exposed, being secreted in a sheltered retreat where the beck, some distance below, runs through a particularly steep-sided length of dale. From here the hitherto parallel road forsakes the valley and climbs rapidly to almost 2000 feet on Fleet Moss before descending to Wensleydale.

To the east of the farm buildings, Oughtershaw Hall stands rather aloof, and looks considerably older than its mid-19th century origins.

Nethergill's appearance is rather an austere one, much in keeping with its surroundings.

At the top end of Oughtershaw are two simple stone memorials to Queen Victoria.

■ STOP PRESS: Plans to create a 600-plus acre forest virtually engulfing Cam Houses and our route overleaf appear to have been fended off, or, highly appropriately, placed where the sun doesn't shine.

The Wharfe at New House, Deepdale

DEEPDALE to NETHERGILL

The Route

Having crossed Deepdale Bridge a wide path sets off along the western bank of the Wharfe, well-defined between wall and river. The attendant wall finally parts company at a stile: continue upstream (with the parallel road also having departed) on a sketchy path to shortly arrive at Beckermonds.

A wooden footbridge takes us over the beck, and a short, walled way leads up to Beckermond's access road. Turn right along it to meet the valley road again. A good mile of road walking now ensues, steeply at first and then undulating through the hamlet of Oughtershaw.

After Oughtershaw's last building the road turns to climb again, but at last we can leave it by continuing along the wide access track straight ahead. It leads first past the farmstead of Nethergill and on still further.

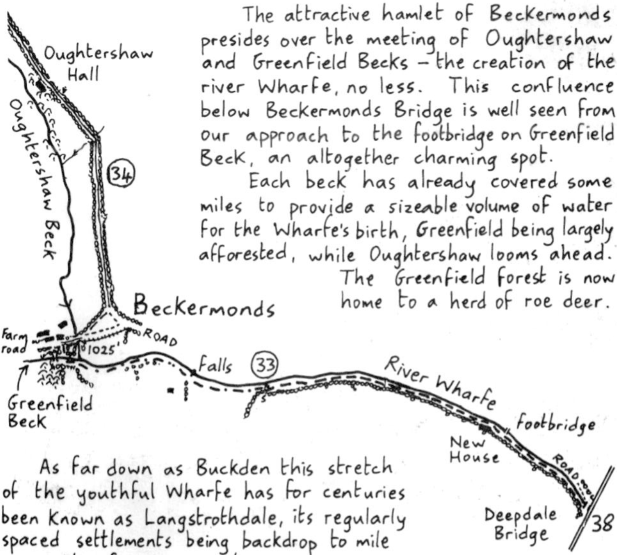

The attractive hamlet of Beckermonds presides over the meeting of Oughtershaw and Greenfield Becks – the creation of the river Wharfe, no less. This confluence below Beckermonds Bridge is well seen from our approach to the footbridge on Greenfield Beck, an altogether charming spot.

Each beck has already covered some miles to provide a sizeable volume of water for the Wharfe's birth, Greenfield being largely afforested, while Oughtershaw looms ahead.

The Greenfield forest is now home to a herd of roe deer.

As far down as Buckden this stretch of the youthful Wharfe has for centuries been known as Langstrothdale, its regularly spaced settlements being backdrop to mile upon mile of unsurpassed river scenery.

The Route

The access track past Nethergill finally expires on arrival at the next farmstead, Swarthgill. Here go left around the buildings and across the small pasture behind to a gate. The same course is now resumed on a sketchy path, the left-hand wall remaining close at hand as three intervening stiles are encountered.

In the next pasture a small barn is passed and in the far corner Breadpiece Barn is reached. After stiles in front and then to its right, the short pull up to Cam Houses begins. A path rises half-right across two pastures before it levels out to run along to the cluster of buildings.

From the stile into their midst turn right through a gate after the first building, then turn left after a gate just above. Behind the other buildings the surfaced access road departs steeply up to the right, but our route keeps straight on, left of the last barn to a gate. Just behind it is a stile in a very short walled section leading into a field: rise diagonally across it towards the top corner of a plantation.

A stile in a fence admits to the plantation, then climb by the trees to meet a wide forestry track. A path now slants away from it up to the left to join a near-parallel fence, which is then followed to the left. Cross it at a stile, and within a few yards the now-sketchy path resumes its rise to soon arrive at a cairn and guidepost alongside the wide course of the Cam High Road.

A bunk barn at Cam Houses is now closed.

HAWES
38
Cam Houses
1450'
Breadpiece Barn
Cam High Road
45
1710'

The lonely farming hamlet of Cam Houses is/are the highest buildings encountered on the walk, and look out across vast miles of bleak Pennine terrain. These uplands of Oughtershaw and Cam Fell have not been improved by the dark cloak of forestry in their midst. Cam Houses' situation is not so isolated as might appear: a line of telegraph poles guide us towards it, while a surfaced road connects with that to Hawes.

NETHERGILL to CAM HIGH ROAD

Cam Houses

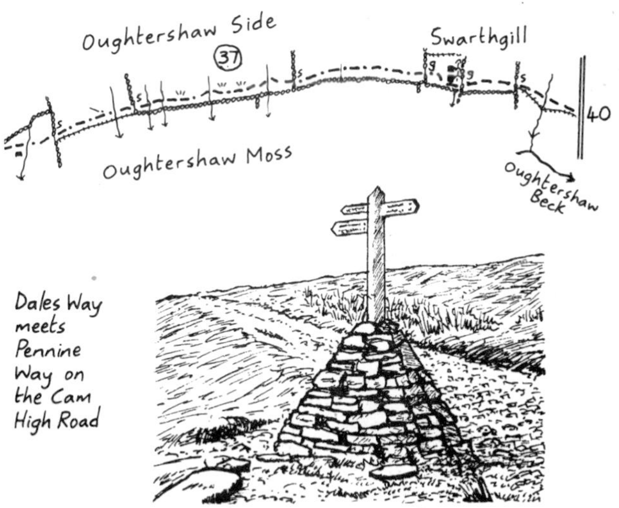

Dales Way meets Pennine Way on the Cam High Road

At Far Gearstones

Penyghent from Winshaw

The Cam High Road is the Roman road that led from Ingleton to their fort at Bainbridge in Wensleydale, and this side of Gearstones it forms an exhilarating high-level march, largely free from motor traffic. In the 1750's the route became a turnpike, but the gentler course through Widdale to Hawes soon took over, the road now classed as the B6255. Gearstones itself, just south of Far Gearstones, once served as a welcome hostelry.

47
High Gayle
42
Winshaw
Holme Hill
HAWES B6255
Gayle Beck
41
milestone
RIBBLEHEAD B6255
Far Gearstones
40
guidepost
Cam End 1430'

A rough descent, the views being ample compensation.

On Cam End the Dales Way concludes its brief association with the Pennine Way.

CAM HIGH ROAD to HIGH GAYLE

The Route

On joining the Cam High Road turn left along it for a near-level march of well over a mile to another cairn and a major fork. Our chosen route is to the right, on a stony course which descends to eventually arrive at a high footbridge over Gayle Beck. Cross to a stile just beyond and then up a short track onto the Ingleton-Hawes road.

After only a couple of minutes along to the left the road is forsaken for a wide track to the right, which rises to the houses at Winshaw. As the track ends continue up with the right-hand wall, turning right with it at the top corner on a clearer path. Remain on this near-level course until the wall drops away just beyond High Gayle Farm below. Here keep straight on to join and turn left along a better track.

From the Cam High Road the 'Three Peaks' of Yorkshire - Penyghent, Ingleborough and Whernside - are major features of the view ahead.

On approaching Cam End the ill-fated Batty Moss Viaduct, Ribblehead appears, from this distance dwarved by mighty Whernside, at 2414 feet, the summit of the Dales.

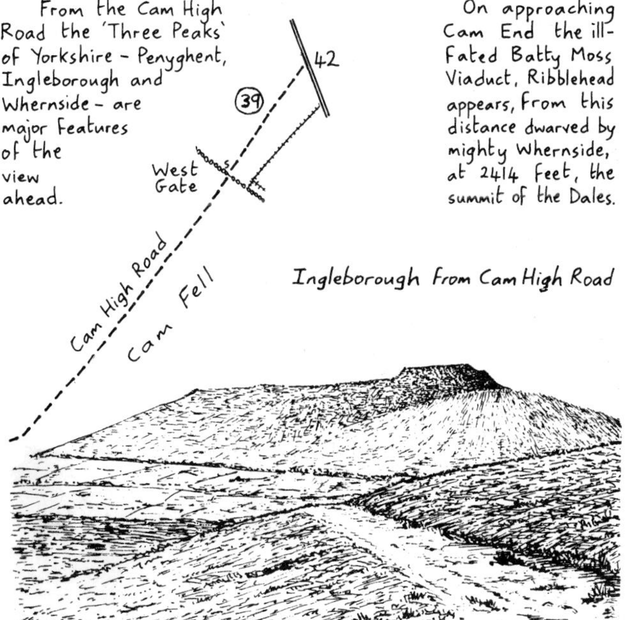

Ingleborough from Cam High Road

Remember the S and C ?

The 72-mile Settle-Carlisle railway was completed in 1876, after seven incredibly hard years when Victorian endeavour reached new heights to battle against Pennine terrain and weather. It was the work of the Midland Railway who were determined to create their own main line through to Scotland. With more sensible routes to east and west, they resorted to facing the challenge of the high Pennines.

Bridges of two eras, Dent Head

Logical approaches via Ribblesdale and the Eden valley led to the central massif from Ribblehead to Mallerstang, and this gave rise to the many spectacular feats of engineering we see today. Deep tunnels alternate with tall viaducts, and the Dales Wayfarer is fortunate in seeing the three greatest viaducts.

During the construction work, thousands of 'navvies' arrived from around the country, and extensive shanty towns sprang up to cater for them. With an air of the Wild West these were lively places, and with little else on which to spend money, numerous well frequented and equally temporary inns witnessed regular outbreaks of violence. Through illnesses like smallpox and construction accidents, churchyards at Chapel-le-Dale and Cowgill were literally overflowing.

The Settle-Carlisle story now moves on a full century, to witness efforts to close the line which ultimately proved even keener than those to open it...... The railway killers were not prepared for an equally determined defence of 'England's Greatest Scenic Railway' by an outraged public : a reasoned, eloquently-argued case for the line's retention, based on common sense and hard facts - not merely enthusiasts' nostalgia - was so strong and well-supported that the dark days since the death knell are ones of incredulity.

Against all expectations, the Settle-Carlisle has been consigned to the scrapheap. Any future it may have would seem to be outside the national rail network, and a 'toytown' pleasure line - without *real* services - is the best we can look forward to.

By the time you read this, it could be the end of the tunnel.

HIGH GAYLE to DENT HEAD

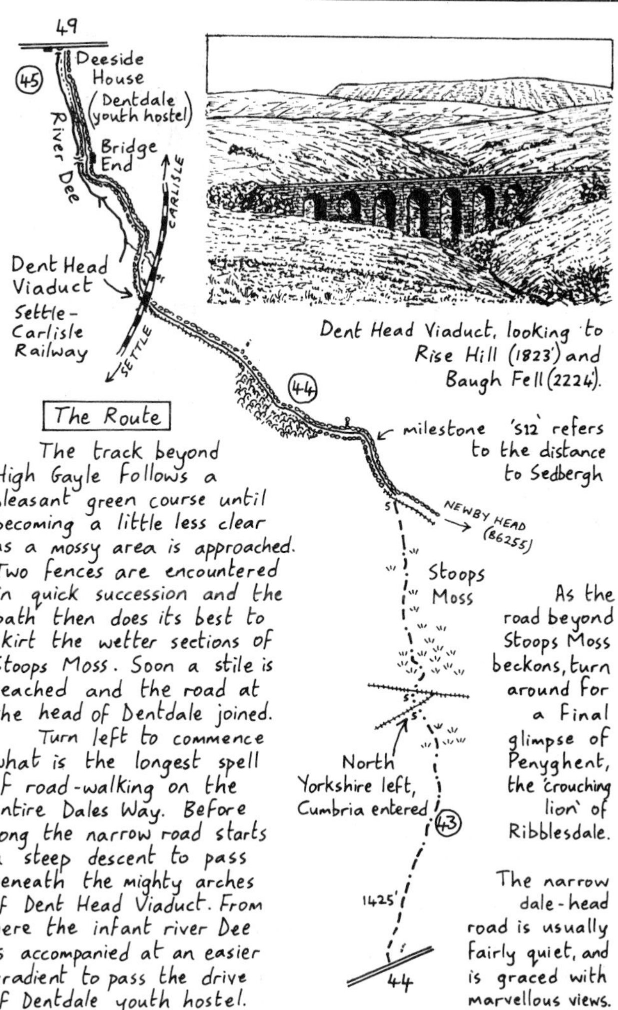

Dent Head Viaduct, looking to Rise Hill (1823') and Baugh Fell (2224').

The Route

The track beyond High Gayle follows a pleasant green course until becoming a little less clear as a mossy area is approached. Two fences are encountered in quick succession and the path then does its best to skirt the wetter sections of Stoops Moss. Soon a stile is reached and the road at the head of Dentdale joined.

Turn left to commence what is the longest spell of road-walking on the entire Dales Way. Before long the narrow road starts a steep descent to pass beneath the mighty arches of Dent Head Viaduct. From here the infant river Dee is accompanied at an easier gradient to pass the drive of Dentdale youth hostel.

As the road beyond Stoops Moss beckons, turn around for a final glimpse of Penyghent, the 'crouching lion' of Ribblesdale.

The narrow dale-head road is usually fairly quiet, and is graced with marvellous views.

SECTION 4

DENT HEAD TO SEDBERGH

12 miles — 500 feet of ascent

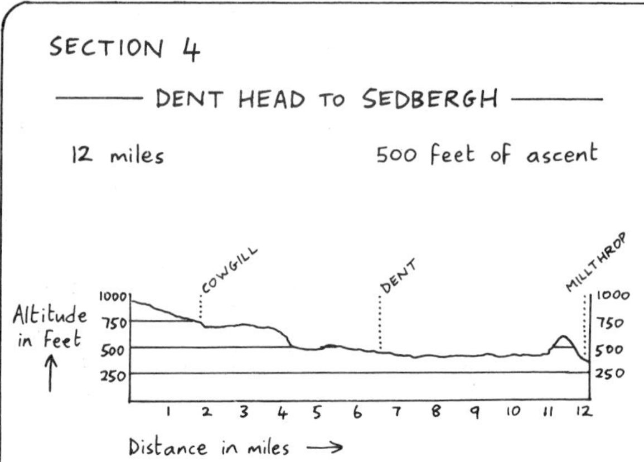

A full length traverse of Dentdale makes for a very easy day slotted appropriately in between the two longest days. This section in any case merits a steady pace, with characterful Dent midway and Sedbergh to enjoy at the end. A substantial amount of minor road walking takes little away from the joys of the Dee, its banks also lending much support. The final miles lead out of Dentdale to descend to the Rawthey, a magnificent backdrop of the Howgill Fells providing a fitting ending.

Millthrop Bridge

DENT HEAD to COWGILL

The Route

After Dentdale youth hostel the road remains our chosen course, with the Dee always in close proximity. At Stone House the river is crossed, the inn is passed, and soon Lea Yeat Bridge is reached, where the road returns to the opposite bank, to Cowgill.

The river Dee is a lively, sparkling watercourse, swift flowing and crystal clear. Here in the upper dale it tumbles over countless limestone ledges, and in dry weather is liable to disappear for substantial lengths. Its grassy and usually tree-lined banks bear nothing larger than a hamlet - Cowgill to be precise!

GARSDALE
Cowgill
51
River Dee
46
inn
Cow Dub
Stone House
limekiln
River Dee
Scow
Scow Force
Deeside House
47

Attractively sited by the river, the youth hostel at Deeside House is a former shooting lodge.

Stone House was the site of a sizeable 19th century marble works, with two mills here. Rising immediately behind is the Artengill Viaduct, constructed of this local black 'Dent marble'. One arch longer than neighbouring Dent Head, it strides a particularly steep-sided and rugged gill.

A former railway navvies' inn

SPORTSMANS INN

The Sportsmans, Cow Dub

The Route

At Lea Yeat Bridge we finally forsake the road in favour of a footpath which keeps us on the southern bank, clinging to the river to soon arrive at Ewegales Bridge. Here turn left up the narrow back road, passing Ewegales Farm and shortly after it taking a gate on the left. An access track rises from it, but is soon left to cross to the farm buildings of Rivling: pass beneath them to run along to a stile into a plantation.

A path flounders through the trees to approach Little Town, whose occupant's privacy has been retained by diverting the path through several stiles to pass round to the right of the buildings. Cross over the access track and straight across to another stile into the second half of the plantation. At the end the path rises to two stiles to escape the trees, then continues alongside a wall to meet another access track beyond a stile. Head up it a few yards and then branch right to cross to a stile, continuing across to meet the access track to Hackergill and Coat Faw.

continued across

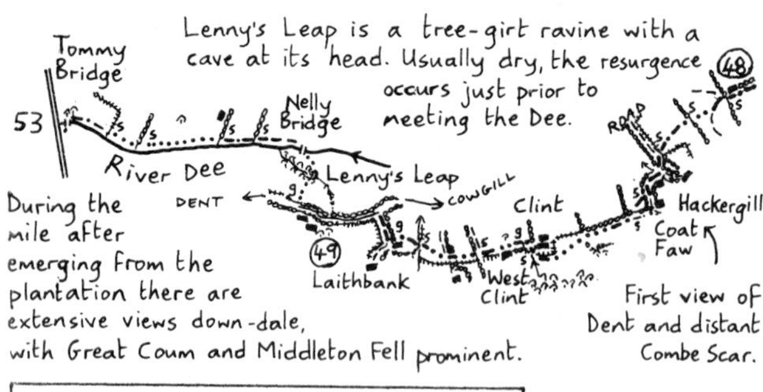

Lenny's Leap is a tree-girt ravine with a cave at its head. Usually dry, the resurgence occurs just prior to meeting the Dee.

During the mile after emerging from the plantation there are extensive views down-dale, with Great Coum and Middleton Fell prominent.

First view of Dent and distant Combe Scar.

Middleton Fell, Combe Scar and Helms Knott from West Clint

COWGILL to TOMMY BRIDGE

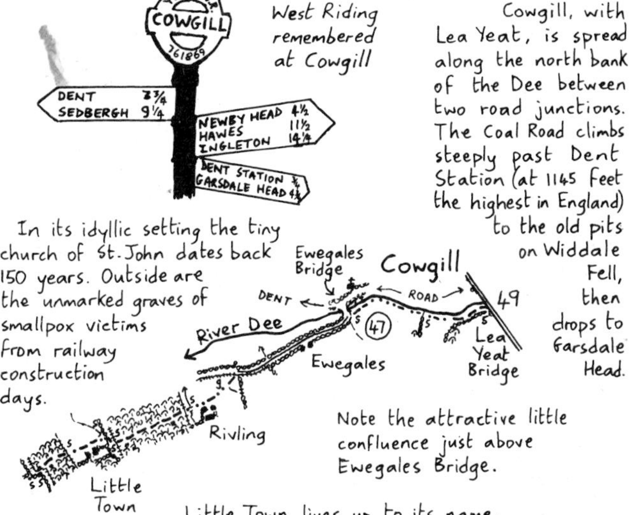

West Riding remembered at Cowgill

Cowgill, with Lea Yeat, is spread along the north bank of the Dee between two road junctions. The Coal Road climbs steeply past Dent Station (at 1145 feet the highest in England) to the old pits on Widdale Fell, then drops to Garsdale Head.

In its idyllic setting the tiny church of St. John dates back 150 years. Outside are the unmarked graves of smallpox victims from railway construction days.

Note the attractive little confluence just above Ewegales Bridge.

Little Town lives up to its name.

The Route continued

Turn left along the access track and immediately fork right over a beck to see a stile on the right. From it cross a field to the next stile then turn right with the wall below a prominent scar. On approaching Clint we are deflected above its confines by a fence before dropping to a stile and gate to resume a level walk with a wall now on the left. Pass by West Clint and at the field-corner leave its access track at a stile, continuing on past a barn and along to cross a small beck. Just beyond it go to the right of a large barn, and from the gate there turn down Laithbank's access track to join a road.

Go left along this back road last seen at Ewegales, until just past the house on the left, then take a gate into a field on the right. Cross to the prominent wooded confines of Lenny's Leap, passing to the right to arrive at the river Dee once more, and Nelly Bridge. Cross this footbridge and turn downstream, encountering several stiles before very shortly reaching the next footbridge, Tommy Bridge.

Dent is only a village in size, but historically is known as Dent Town. Until fairly recently it was of greater importance than Sedbergh, but today it is an unhurried backwater. Dent stands midway along its own valley, and the only roads in and out are minor ones, a factor which has helped preserve Dent's character. Retained are some cobbled streets lined with neat cottages, a few shops, a brace of inns and a lovely church, 15th century but restored a century ago.

By the side of the main street is a block of Shap granite made into a drinking fountain carved with the name of Adam Sedgwick. Born here in 1785, he went off to Cambridge and spent over 50 years as Professor of Geology. He was one of the earliest and best geologists, and did much research into the varied geology of his own back yard. The bicentenary of his birth was commemorated by the creation of an appropriate trail in neighbouring Garsdale.

TOMMY BRIDGE to DENT

55 COWGILL Church Bridge
River Dee
Dent
51
Deepdale Beck
R. Dee
50
550'
viewpoint
DENT
Mill Bridge
COWGILL

※ This modest little brow above the river is an outstanding Dentdale viewpoint, being surrounded by varied fell country. Illustrated are the three mountains on parade:-
left: Widdale Fell (2203')
top: Whernside (2414')
bottom: Great Coum (2253')

The Route

At Tommy Bridge cross the Dee again and continue downstream, but at only the second gate make use of a stile on the left, leaving the river to climb by a right-hand wall. At the top head directly away to descend to a stile by a cottage, then go right along the lane to Mill Bridge.

Across the bridge go into the trees on the right, on a path which shadows Deepdale Beck down to its confluence with the Dee. The river takes us downstream again, and just prior to Church Bridge we are deflected by the flood embankment to cross a stream, then following it right to meet the road.

Dent is now only two minutes up to the left.

Barth Bridge

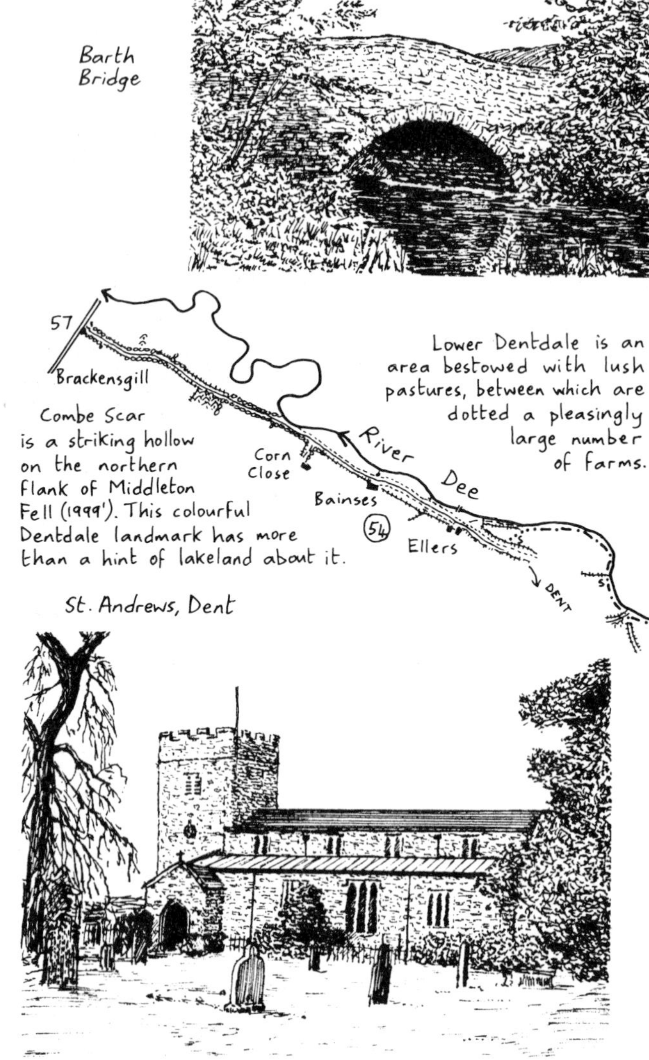

Lower Dentdale is an area bestowed with lush pastures, between which are dotted a pleasingly large number of farms.

Combe Scar is a striking hollow on the northern flank of Middleton Fell (1999'). This colourful Dentdale landmark has more than a hint of lakeland about it.

St. Andrews, Dent

DENT to BRACKENSGILL

Church Bridge, Dent, with Middleton Fell beyond

Footpath signs at both Church and Barth Bridges point the way to Hippins: what and where is it?

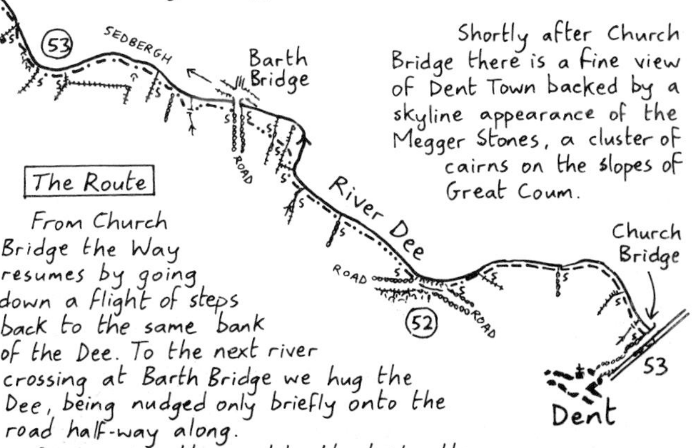

Shortly after Church Bridge there is a fine view of Dent Town backed by a skyline appearance of the Megger Stones, a cluster of cairns on the slopes of Great Coum.

The Route

From Church Bridge the Way resumes by going down a flight of steps back to the same bank of the Dee. To the next river crossing at Barth Bridge we hug the Dee, being nudged only briefly onto the road half-way along.

On crossing the road by the bridge things continue in the same fashion until an enclosing fence is met with Ellers footbridge just ahead - here bear left to a stile to cross a mini-swamp onto a road. Turn right along this lovely back road, past the footbridge and on in undisturbed peace.

Sedbergh is the largest community in the Yorkshire Dales National Park, yet its isolation has helped it avoid the excesses of commercialism. Ceded to Cumbria in 1974, Sedbergh - omit the last two letters in pronunciation - was previously in the north-western extremity of the West Riding of Yorkshire, incredibly over 100 miles distant from its West Riding colleague Sheffield. Two simple facts prove that size is very much a relative thing.

This tiny market town boasts an unparalleled position on the lower slopes of its 'own' mountains the Howgill Fells, and the outlook on three sides is, in fact, of fells. This is the edge of the Dales, and to the west of the town runs the river Lune. In the neighbourhood of Sedbergh three lively rivers end their journeys, as the Dee, Clough and Rawthey join forces to swell the waters of the Lune.

Aside from the imposing Howgill Fells, Sedbergh itself is dominated by its public school. This famous establishment, which was founded in the early 16th century, includes Adam Sedgwick (see page 52) among its old boys. The oldest remaining part dates from 1716, and is now the library. Most other features of interest will be found on or near the lengthy main street, including a lovely parish church in an equally attractive wooded surround. Dedicated to St. Andrew it has a 15th century tower, with other parts dating back to Norman times as well as many other periods in between.

St. Andrew's Sedbergh

BRACKENSGILL to SEDBERGH

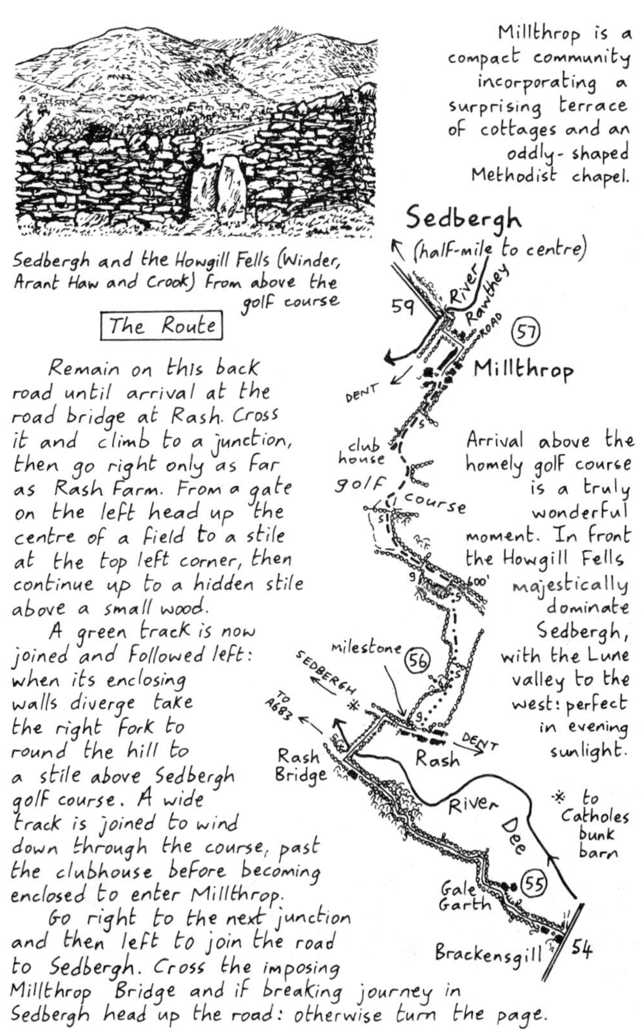

Sedbergh and the Howgill Fells (Winder, Arant Haw and Crook) from above the golf course

Millthrop is a compact community incorporating a surprising terrace of cottages and an oddly-shaped Methodist chapel.

Arrival above the homely golf course is a truly wonderful moment. In front the Howgill Fells majestically dominate Sedbergh, with the Lune valley to the west: perfect in evening sunlight.

The Route

Remain on this back road until arrival at the road bridge at Rash. Cross it and climb to a junction, then go right only as far as Rash Farm. From a gate on the left head up the centre of a field to a stile at the top left corner, then continue up to a hidden stile above a small wood.

A green track is now joined and followed left: when its enclosing walls diverge take the right fork to round the hill to a stile above Sedbergh golf course. A wide track is joined to wind down through the course, past the clubhouse before becoming enclosed to enter Millthrop.

Go right to the next junction and then left to join the road to Sedbergh. Cross the imposing Millthrop Bridge and if breaking journey in Sedbergh head up the road: otherwise turn the page.

SECTION 5

SEDBERGH TO BURNESIDE

17 miles 1300 feet of ascent

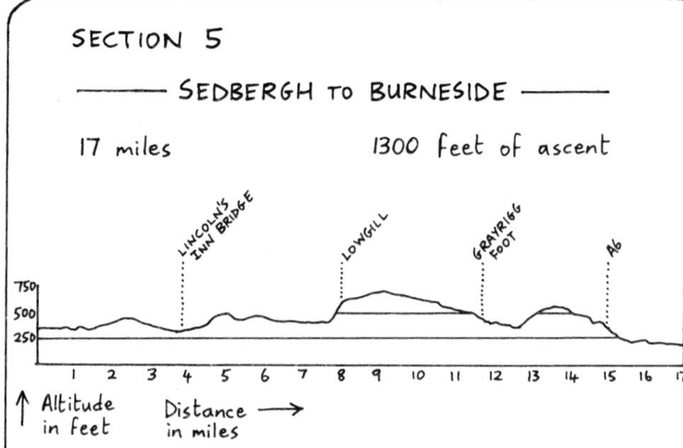

This longest day is one of immense variety as we traverse the undulating country twixt Dales and Lakes. The ever lively Lune guides us beneath the slopes of the Howgill Fells before green pastures lead to the rivers Mint, Sprint and ultimately the Kent at Burneside. The no-mans-land between the National Parks supports few villages, and refreshment opportunities are sparse: ensure everything for the day is carried. A feature of the day is the prospect of fells to all points but south, with lakeland's fells slowly replacing the Howgills. Immediately north, Whinfell's ridge rises above the anomolies of the current Park boundaries.

Allow a *full* day for this section - although route-finding is not difficult, it can be time-consuming.

Morning mist leaving Winder, from Bruce Loch

SEDBERGH to BRIGFLATTS

The Route

After crossing Millthrop Bridge the Way leaves the road almost immediately at a kissing-gate after a drive on the left. Swing to the right around the field and take a gate into the wood at the far end. Head along the fairly level path which soon swings right at a curious walled trench to leave the wood at another kissing-gate. Turn left with the fence, passing right of a ruinous little edifice to drop down the field towards the river Rawthey.

Head upstream a short way before the path rises to the left of a house to emerge onto a narrow lane. Go left along it, by the houses at Birks to its demise at Birks Mill. The riverbank is regained here and it remains in close company all the way to Brigflatts, the next settlement. A brief interruption is caused by a former railway line which the path must surmount.

Below Birks Mill the river Dee comes to bid farewell at its delightful tree-lined confluence.

SEDBERGH
Enterprising nature reserve
Birks
Bruce Loch
(58)
57
Birks Mill
former cotton mill
61
River Rawthey
River Dee
old railway bridge

x = a ruined tower on a prominent knoll, providing one of the best local views of the Howgill Fells.

At Birks Mill a high footbridge spans the Rawthey and serves as a useful vantage point for some splendid river scenery. Note the former mill-race by the path immediately downstream.

The next bridge down-river is a vastly different one, a single-arched iron structure looking strangely out of place since it lost its purpose. The Ingleton-Tebay branch railway once steamed high above the Rawthey, but this sad reminder is now unsafe, and access barred. The old track bed still aims north to the Howgills, and is soon encountered more spectacularly. The northern panorama from here includes, clockwise, Firbank Fell, Howgill Fells (southern), Baugh Fell and Frostrow Fells.

Friends Meeting House, Brigflatts

Dating from the seventeenth century and one of the oldest Quaker establishments in the country, it is still put to its original use. It can be located from the path, beyond the farm buildings.

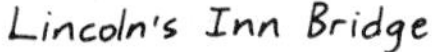

Lincoln's Inn Bridge

BRIGFLATTS to LINCOLN'S INN BRIDGE

A shapely but disconcerting aspect for several miles is that of Winder (1553'), nearest of the Howgill Fells: it never seems to recede into the distance to suggest we're actually making any progress!

The only disappointment with the Rawthey is that we don't spend enough time with it. This gem of a watercourse remains untainted throughout its short life, from 2000 feet up on the top of Baugh Fell, around the feet of the Howgills to its absorption into the Lune just after we take our leave. It can be followed on foot for almost all its length.

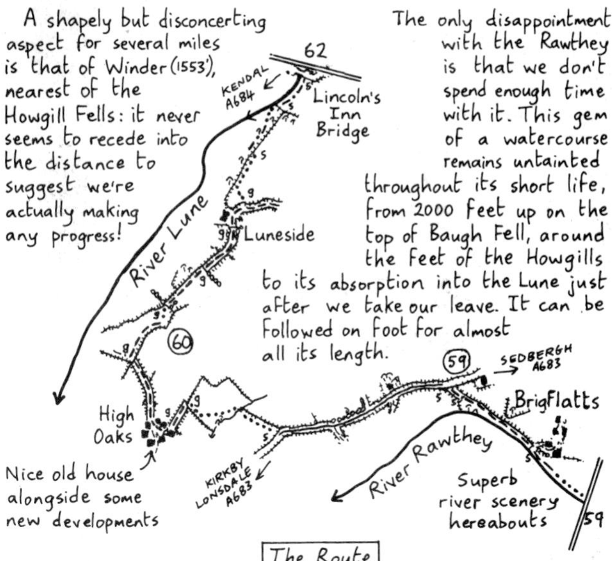

The Route

The Way clings to the river as Brigflatts' farm buildings are passed, but when the Rawthey makes a wide swing away the fenced path continues straight on to join the A683. Go left for under half a mile and take a stile on the right (to High Oaks). Follow the fence away to cross a tiny stream, then rise half-left over a knoll to join the fence across to the left. Turn right with it to a gate in the far corner then go left along a delightful green way to enter the confines of High Oaks.

Turn right after the farmhouse to leave along a pleasant hedged track: at its demise at a gate take the track to the right, passing by a stile and continuing on to a gate at the far end. A wide track now leads directly to Luneside farm. After the buildings leave its access track by a gate on the left, then cross to a fence and follow it away to a stile in it. Now head across towards the river Lune to accompany it upstream to Lincoln's Inn Bridge, just ahead.

Crook of Lune Bridge is a genuinely beautiful structure, inclined and narrow, and it marks our exit from the Dales National Park. Until 1974 it spanned the West Riding of Yorkshire and Westmorland border. Of ancient origin it is fortunate in seeing little more than local traffic, yet half a mile away vehicles thunder past on the motorway.

The river Lune rises 1700 feet up on the Howgill Fells, and after skirting their base it heads for Lancaster and its own county. We see it very much in its infancy, though it remains equally untainted almost to the sea. To follow its full course would make a fine expedition.

From the vicinity of Bramaskew the chapel at Firbank, across the river, can be easily located. On the fell above is 'Fox's pulpit', where in 1652 George Fox's great speech, after his Pendle Hill vision, founded the Quaker movement.

The Lune Viaduct's appearance is a dramatic one, its red sandstone arches rising powerfully above a pastoral scene. It is the second of three we encounter from the defunct Ingleton-Tebay line, and its top (bridge section barricaded) boasts extensive Lune valley and western Howgill panoramas

The unevenly arched but highly attractive Lincoln's Inn Bridge recalls a former hostelry that occupied the far bank: only a farm remains. Never mind, the next surviving one is only ?※! miles distant, at Burneside!

On the approach to Chapel Beck we encounter the river at close quarters, with a wide, stony bank leading the eye to Fell Head, in the Howgills.

63
Chapel Beck
(63)
Thwaite (farm)
Smithy Beck
Hole House (farm)
※ viewpoint on brow (see overleaf)
450'
Nether Bainbridge (farm)
River Lune
(62)
Bramaskew (farm)
Low Branthwaite (farm)
Lune Viaduct
Crosdale Beck
Ford
Map extended to show alternative path to Low Branthwaite if ford impassable.
(61)
Lincoln's Inn Bridge
61
SEDBERGH A684

LINCOLN'S INN BRIDGE to CROOK OF LUNE BRIDGE

A surplus of interesting features (along with bad page management!) has resulted in the next two pages being seconded to this particular section.

The Route

From Lincoln's Inn Bridge cross the A684 to a gate to resume the walk up the Lune's eastern bank. The Lune Viaduct soon looms ahead, and the Way passes beneath its tall arches before leaving the river to rise up the field. The path swings right and then fades before crossing the now-level pasture to a stile, with a beck just down to the right. A track now heads away to arrive at Low Branthwaite.

Cross straight over its access track from stile to stile and follow the left-hand fence away. Turn right at the corner to rise up the field, a track materialising to become briefly enclosed. On emerging, ignore the obvious track to Bramaskew Farm straight ahead, but cross to a gap-stile just to its left. Head away past the farm to another stile, then descend a large field to a small barn. A track commences and becomes enclosed to lead to Nether Bainbridge.

Without entering its confines take a stile before a barn on the left, going past the barn and then turning left with the facing wall. Use a gate at a bend in it to climb to a little brow, continuing across to descend to Hole House Farm. From the gate in front enter its yard, turning right past the barns and then forking left to pass along the private-looking way between dwellinghouses to a small gate.

A footbridge crosses Smithy Beck and the lower of two paths leads to a stile on the left. Now cross to the river to accompany the Lune through a large pasture below Thwaite Farm. Another footbridge is crossed and the way remains clear, staying with the river until a gate below Crook of Lune Farm up to the right. Follow the track which meets a wider one to then join a narrow lane descending to Crook of Lune Bridge.

Lune Viaduct

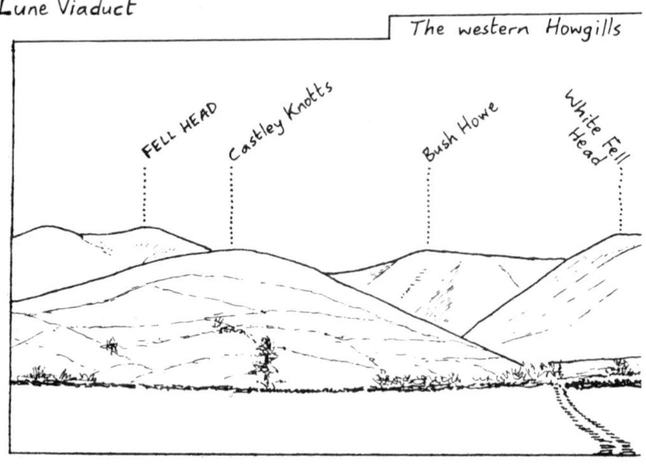

The western Howgills

Crook of Lune Bridge

From above Hole House

THE CALF

Bram Rigg Top

Calders

The Route

On crossing Crook of Lune Bridge the narrow lane soon begins a short, steep climb, passing below the Lowgill Viaduct to a T-junction. Go right and then immediately left to then leave the road by turning up the front of the lone house on the left. An enclosed way rises to a stile and a sharp bend: here go straight ahead by a line of trees, and at some intervening trees graduate to the field top. From a stile at the far corner remain level, a track soon appearing to run along to join the drive to Lakethwaite farm.

Head briefly up it then take a stile on the right before the first building, to skirt the outside of its confines. Initially climbing, follow a wall then a fence directly away to a stile in the field corner. In the next field corner a stile admits to a quiet road: turn up it for a few yards then opt for a stile on the right. Follow the wall heading away, and from a gate in a bend in it, head for a farm bridge across the gracefully curving M6 motorway.

continued across

Grayrigg village increasingly features ahead.

Moresdale Hall is an uninspiring looking mansion usurped by the more appealing house a little before it, alongside a fine wooded beck.

Lambrigg Head marks the important Lune-Kent watershed crossing.

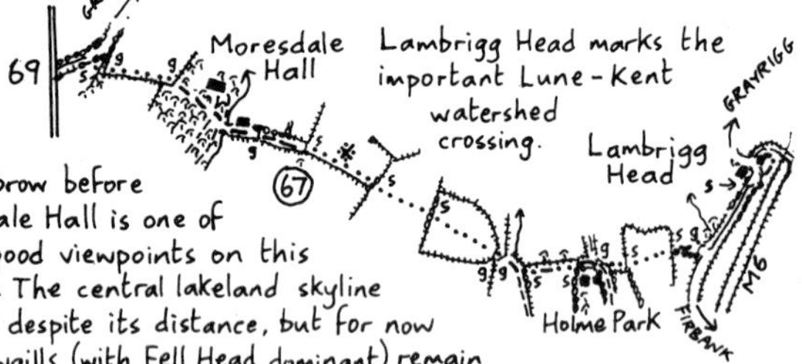

※ The brow before Moresdale Hall is one of many good viewpoints on this section. The central lakeland skyline excites despite its distance, but for now the Howgills (with Fell Head dominant) remain more tangible. *North-west, however, is lakeland's eastern fringe.....*

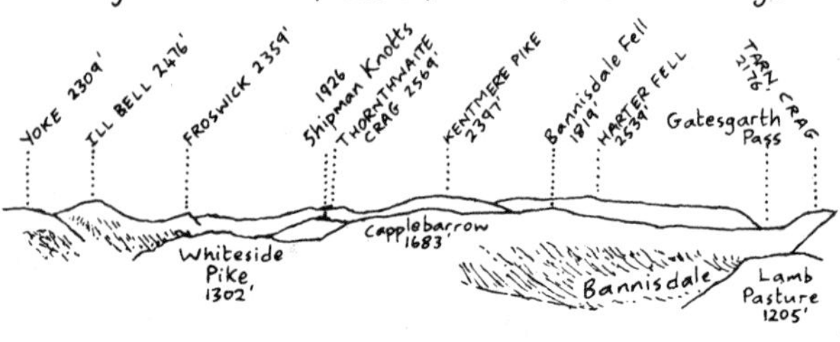

CROOK OF LUNE BRIDGE to MORESDALE HALL

The Route continued

Instead of following the track down to Lambrigg Head, go immediately left to pass between motorway fence and farm buildings to a stile onto a narrow road. Go left and leave it by a gate on the right after it has widened. Head half-left to a stile and then directly away along a groove to the next stile. Continue on to a gate and along a drive to the right of the buildings at Home Park.

Keep on to a stile and along a field bottom to a stile onto a green track. Go right to two successive gates, then cross a field by dropping a little to a stile in a wall opposite. Do the same in the next field to accompany a left-hand fence away over a gentle brow. The next stile gains a pleasant, enclosed path to the environs of Moresdale Hall.

After the first house a bridge is crossed: instead of following the drive, then bear half-right up a slope to a parallel drive with the hall just to the right. Again keep straight on along a clear path through the trees. On emerging remain with the left-hand fence to cross a tiny beck before rising to a stile onto a lane.

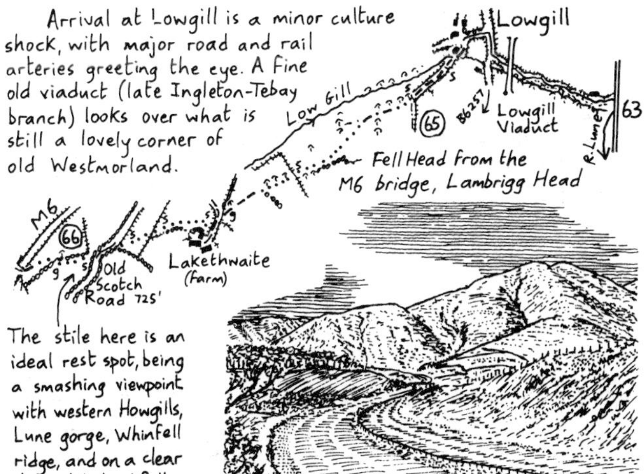
Arrival at Lowgill is a minor culture shock, with major road and rail arteries greeting the eye. A fine old viaduct (late Ingleton-Tebay branch) looks over what is still a lovely corner of old Westmorland.
Lowgill
Low Gill
65
B6257
Lowgill Viaduct
63
R. Lune
M6
66
Old Scotch Road 725'
Lakethwaite (farm)
The stile here is an ideal rest spot, being a smashing viewpoint with western Howgills, Lune gorge, Whinfell ridge, and on a clear day.... lakeland fells.

Fell Head from the M6 bridge, Lambrigg Head

The river Mint's appearance is an unexpected but very welcome one. Though we pass like ships in the night, it is not easily forgotten, flowing as it does through the beautiful park-like environs of Shaw End: note the stone arched bridge a few sedately meandering minutes downstream. The Mint begins life as Bannisdale Beck in a deep lakeland valley, and meets its end in the Kent on the edge of Kendal.

On meeting the road above Biglands the availability of duck eggs is overshadowed by a splendid view over the Mint's gathering grounds.

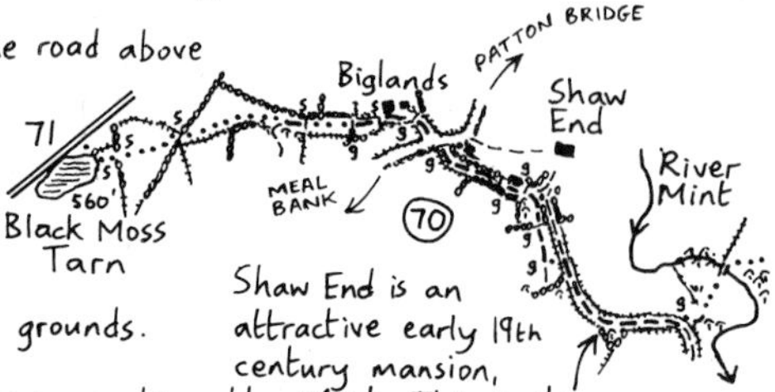

Shaw End is an attractive early 19th century mansion, seen ahead before reaching the Mint. This inviting hedgerowed lane is its old drive.

The Route

Turn left along the narrow road to a junction at Thatchmoor Head, then double back to the right as far as a lone dwelling. Take a gate opposite it and follow the field-top away to approach the railway, dropping to cross with care at a bridle-gate. Head directly away from it to pick up a tractor track in the colourful environs of a small beck. This track soon rises left, becoming enclosed at a gate, then swings left to reach Green Head Farm.

Keep left of the farm buildings and head down the access road, but before a cattle-grid at the bottom bear right on a faint green track to a gate and then a footbridge over a beck. Make for the gate between farm buildings at Grayrigg Foot and then follow the drive out onto the A685. Head up it a few yards and then turn along the farm road towards Thursgill.

After crossing a beck leave the drive by a gate on the left and cross to a hurdle-stile in the corner of the field. A short pull leads to a stile in the next corner, then the left-hand hedge leads over a brow to meet a tractor track. Go right towards a barn but then opt for a gate in the facing hedge. Head directly away - without gaining any height - then bear left to drop down to a footbridge over the river Mint. continued across

MORESDALE HALL to BLACK MOSS TARN

The Route continued

Rise up the field behind to find a kissing-gate onto an enclosed green lane, which is followed up to the right. At the second iron kissing-gate on the left move to a parallel track through the field, and at a gate follow it up to the left to pass through the yard of a house. Just above, it enters a narrow enclosed way to rise onto a road.

Cross straight over and down the drive to Biglands, going left in front of the house to a stile. Head along a narrow pasture to a collapsed wall, and when the field widens beyond keep left to a stile at the end. Head across the next field to another collapsed stile giving access to Black Moss Tarn.

Thursgill
GRAYRIGG A685
Grayrigg (farm) Foot
69
Green Head (farm)
KENDAL A685

A last glimpse of Grayrigg's church tower here, with the repeater station on Whinfell directly behind.

Having been close for so long, the busy west coast main line is finally crossed

CARLISLE
GRAYRIGG (see note)
LANCASTER
68
66
Thatchmoor Head
DOCKER
LAMBRIGG HEAD

NB: If in dire need of some form of civilisation, then by remaining on the road out of Thatchmoor Head (not a barber in sight) the little village of Grayrigg will be gained. To escape the bustle of this metropolis, a short spell on the A685 towards Kendal will pick up the route. Only Grayrigg Foot, of interest, is omitted, while the railway crossing is safely avoided.

Footbridge at Grayrigg Foot ..... a pleasant spot to linger

The Route

From a stile in the short fence running into the tarn, follow its northern bank and climb the field behind to the obtrusive pylon. Descend to New House Farm just below, entering its yard and going left of the house to a small gate. From it an enticing pathway runs – largely enclosed – for some length before meeting the access road to Goodham Scales on the right.

Go left along the road and at a sharp bend left take a gate in front to follow a near-equal road down to Garnett Folds. A quiet access road heads away, passing near Skelsmergh Tarn and by Tarn Bank Farm then concludes with a steep drop to the A6. Cross the road and go left for a few yards, then take the drive to Burton House. Take the gate ahead (left of the house) and one immediately left, then cross a small enclosure to another gate. Now cross the field to a prominent ladder-stile just beyond a marshy area: a short path then runs to a footbridge across the outflow.

continued across

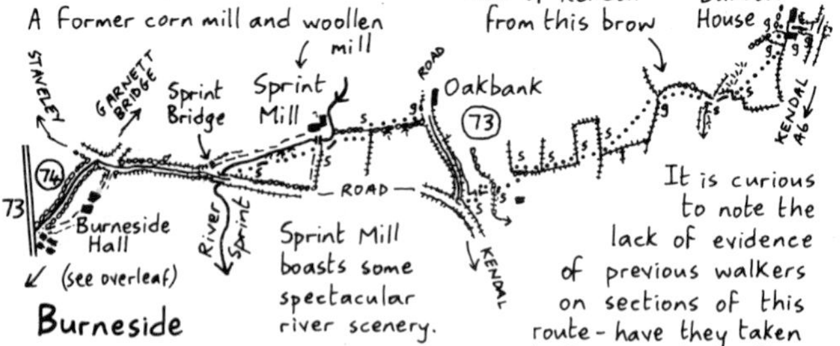

A former corn mill and woollen mill

Sprint Mill boasts some spectacular river scenery.

It is curious to note the lack of evidence of previous walkers on sections of this route - have they taken to the roads for the final miles to Burneside?

The distant lakeland skyline from the descent to Oakbank

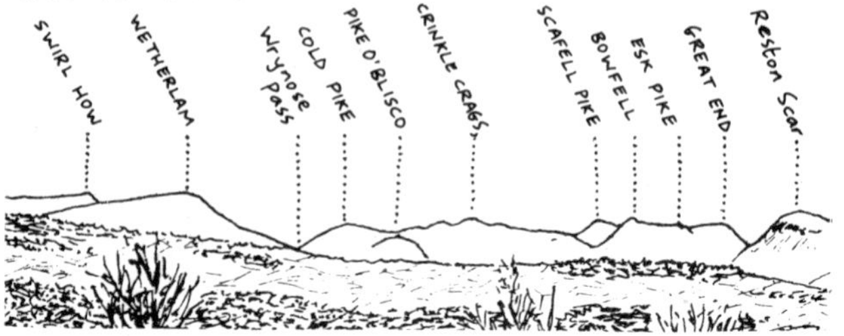

BLACK MOSS TARN to BURNESIDE

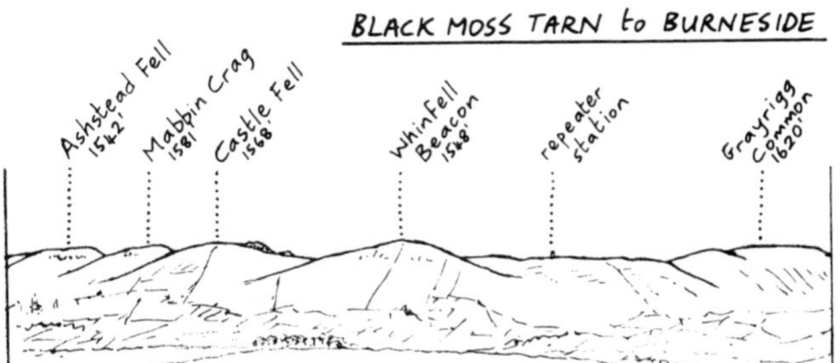

The Whinfell ridge, looking north from above Black Moss Tarn. This green knoll before New House gives a marvellous upland panorama from the Howgills to Lakeland.

Goodham Scales
71
New House
605'
68
pylon
a classic green lane
Black Moss Tarn
ROAD
Good view south to Benson Knott
A6
Skelsmergh Tarn
Garnett Folds
Tarn Bank
72

Tree-shrouded Skelsmergh Tarn may easily be passed by without notice.

The Route continued

Climb straight up the field-side to go through a gate, then drop half-left to a stile in the very corner. Rise to another directly above it, then follow the field-side up and over a modest brow. After an intervening stile look for one in the bottom corner in a short wall-section on the left. Head directly away to the next wall-cum-hedge, and locate a stile where a watercourse meets this field boundary. Follow the stream up to a basic bridge over it then continue on to a stile onto a road junction.

Opt for the lesser road to the right, and leave it by a gate on the left just prior to a terraced row at Oakbank. Follow the wall away to a stile in it, then continue on its other side to meet the river Sprint. Head left along its bank, past the bridge at Sprint Mill and along to a stile onto the road at Sprint Bridge. Turn right along the road and soon after passing Burneside Hall, the road swings left to approach Burneside.

Though the Dales Way doesn't enter the village proper, many will wish to break their journey here, keeping straight on for the main street with its various facilities.

SECTION 6

BURNESIDE TO BOWNESS

10 miles — 1100 feet of ascent

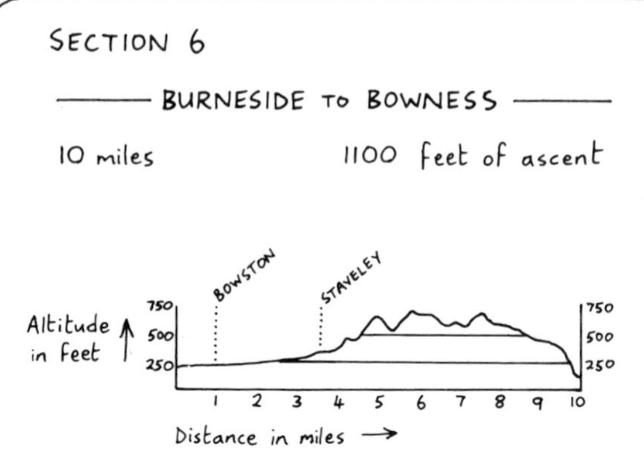

An extremely straightforward day brings the Dales Way to its conclusion, allowing ample time to savour the well-earned delights of Bowness and Windermere. Two more well-defined sections divide these final miles. Firstly the inviting banks of the Kent transport us unfailingly into the Lakes proper, and to Staveley, the only interim village. From here rolling upland pastures take over; typical south lakeland terrain to guide our steps to near Windermere's shores. Frustratingly the lake remains elusive almost to the end, and the route skilfully avoids the hordes for even longer.

Burneside Hall

BURNESIDE to BOWSTON

The Route

Leave the road into Burneside by a stile and then a kissing-gate on the right immediately before the first houses and the mill. Follow the mill's perimeter fence away to another kissing-gate, then go left to meet a mill-race from the Kent. Head upstream past the weir, being briefly deflected away to a stile to escape marshy ground. A field is then crossed to join the river Kent proper, which is then accompanied upstream to steps up to Bowston Bridge.

Cross the bridge and go up the lane to meet the road from Burneside, which is followed along to the right.

Burneside straddles the river Kent, two miles north of Kendal from which it remains happily independent. Equally happily, it has long avoided the lakes-bound traffic on the wide road high above. Although substantially enlarged by modern housing, the village continues to be overshadowed by an enormous paper mill, an important source of employment locally. Whilst not of great antiquity, the parish church of St. Oswald has a solid tower of typical lakeland construction, and its interior boasts some fine woodwork.

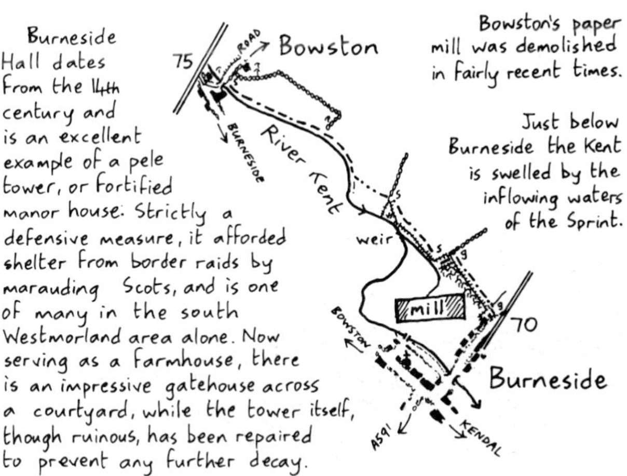

Burneside Hall dates from the 14th century and is an excellent example of a pele tower, or fortified manor house. Strictly a defensive measure, it afforded shelter from border raids by marauding Scots, and is one of many in the south Westmorland area alone. Now serving as a farmhouse, there is an impressive gatehouse across a courtyard, while the tower itself, though ruinous, has been repaired to prevent any further decay.

Bowston's paper mill was demolished in fairly recent times.

Just below Burneside the Kent is swelled by the inflowing waters of the Sprint.

The railway at Staveley is the single-track branch line to Windermere, which leaves the west coast main line at Oxenholme. The Kendal and Windermere Railway was opened in 1847, largely to serve Kendal which was left high and dry by the main line two miles to the east. The railway created Windermere town, for until its coming no more than a hamlet existed there. One of the line's stronger critics was Wordsworth, who feared an invasion of town and city folk: it is ironic that more visitors than he could have imagined now come, but only a tiny proportion use this surviving line.

The sparkling Kent is reputedly our fastest flowing river, maintaining its own identity from the slopes of High Street to its estuary in Morecambe Bay. It belonged entirely to old Westmorland.

At this stile the Lake District National Park is entered, while Burneside's fishing waters are vacated for those of Staveley. Has anyone told the fish? Almost immediately a rock scramble confirms we're in lakeland.

The Route

Remain on the road at Bowston for only a short distance before turning down a pleasant snicket opposite a 'phone box, to pass between houses and rejoin the river at another weir. A level track now heads upstream, merging into a surfaced lane to run along to the environs of Cowen Head. Remain on the road left of the mill buildings, past a 'phone box to two short rows of dwellings. Here the road ends and a path heads across to a gate and the Kent's bank again.

Now head up-dale and remain on the very bank of the river past a farm bridge. Beyond a large barn a clear path runs through a more rugged wooded area, then fades when a wall intervenes to separate us from the Kent. Cross the field from a gateway to a stile in the far corner and regain the river.

Across the next field a narrow, rocky section is encountered, and when the next wall intervenes at a river bend, go right to a gate and continue with a wall between us and the river. At the end a walled track leads directly up to Sandy Hill Farm. Emerging onto the road at the edge of Staveley, go right and then cross to the first buildings on the other side, going up an enclosed track to a railway underpass.

BOWSTON to STAVELEY

Right: Cowen Head Mill

Below: Bowston Bridge

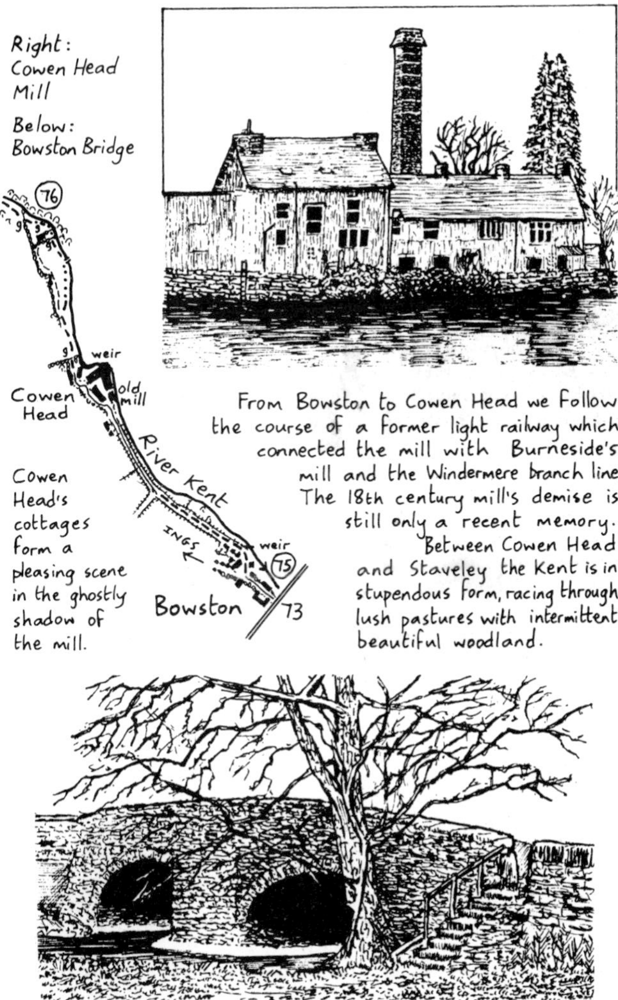

Cowen Head's cottages form a pleasing scene in the ghostly shadow of the mill.

From Bowston to Cowen Head we follow the course of a former light railway which connected the mill with Burneside's mill and the Windermere branch line. The 18th century mill's demise is still only a recent memory.

Between Cowen Head and Staveley the Kent is in stupendous form, racing through lush pastures with intermittent beautiful woodland.

The Route

From the railway underpass opt for the right-hand of the twin tracks branching away. At the field-end it turns left to accompany a wall to Moss Side, then take a stile to emerge by a garage at the front of the buildings. Go out along the drive to emerge onto the Crook road out of Staveley, and head up the road passing under the by-pass.

Part-way up the hill vacate the road by a narrow surfaced drive to Field Close up to the right. At the top turn left to a gate, then up a field to a kissing-gate. Rise up the outside of a wood to the next gate from where a track goes away to join an unfenced road opposite New Hall Farm. Go to the right along this traffic-free back road, which climbs to a brow before descending to a T-junction. Turn right past Fell Plain Farm and uphill again, then near the top go left along a welcoming green bridleway between walls.

continued across

Hag End

Like Outrun Nook, cottage uninhabited

Note this not insubstantial spring which tires of daylight within a couple of yards: the shortest beck encountered just prior to the largest lake.

From the road-top here there is a pleasing view back over the Underbarrow area to the limestone cliffs of Cunswick and Scout Scars.

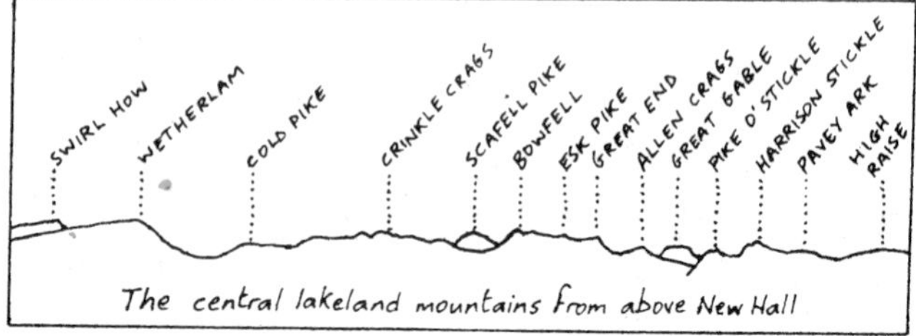

The central lakeland mountains from above New Hall

STAVELEY to HAG END

Staveley is a National Park village that sees little mention in tourist itineraries, but until its rescue by the long-awaited by-pass, millions were squeezed through, bound for the usual haunts. Of interest is the Fifteenth century tower, sole survivor of the old church. Its shops and inns may also demand a few yards detour: there is nothing else before the end. Staveley's own river is not actually the Kent, but the tiny Gowan.

Beyond Staveley the terrain is very typical of this corner of lakeland; little outcrops occuring regularly in these colourful pastures.

Staveley by-pass achieves completion during 1989.

The only signs at the Fell Plain road junction are for the Dales Way path

Above Field Close there are good views back over the village to the fells of Kentmere.

The Route continued

At its terminus take the gate on the right and follow a sketchy track in the same general direction, though bearing steadily away from the wall. From the gate at the far end a better track materialises to skirt the fence of a small plantation: at the bottom vacate the track and accompany a tiny streamlet down to a gate.

Another sketchy track then skirts some gorse bushes to drop down to a stile, from where a fine track then rises towards Crag House Farm. On emerging in front of a large, modern barn turn right along the track rising up towards the farm, but then branch off with the right-hand wall to a facing gate in the wall corner.

Head away down the next field, rounding some trees in the centre to locate a kissing-gate at the bottom and join a quiet road by the farm buildings at Outrun Nook. Turn right for a minute or so and then branch left along the access track to Hag End.

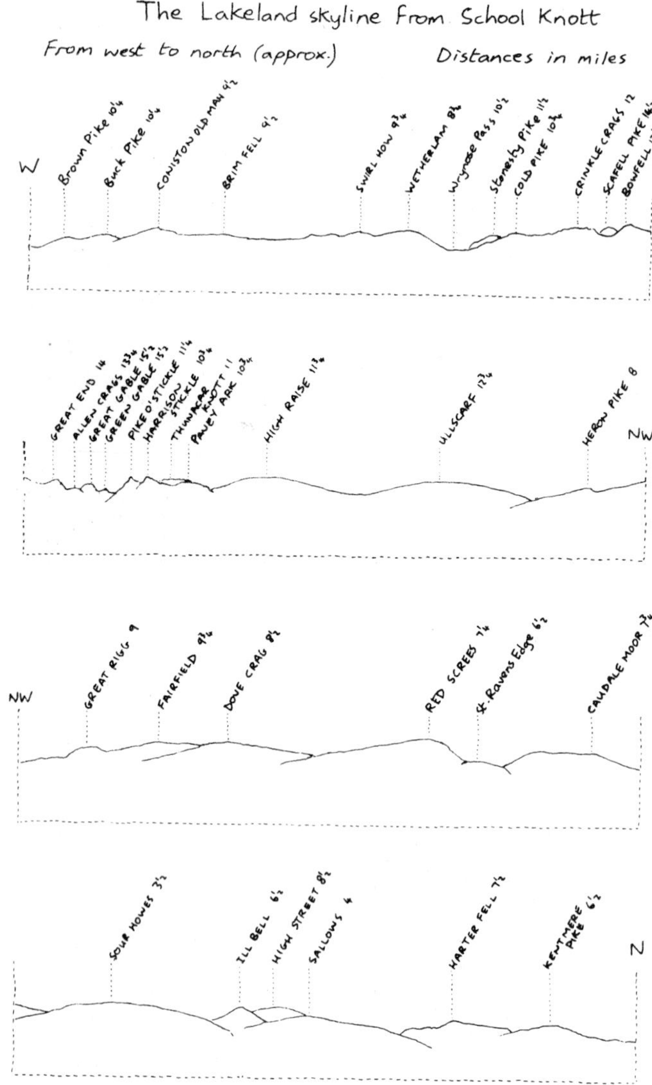
The Lakeland skyline from School Knott
From west to north (approx.)
Distances in miles
W
Brown Pike 10¼
Buck Pike 10¼
CONISTON OLD MAN 9½
BRIM FELL 9½
SWIRL HOW 9¾
WETHERLAM 8¾
Wrynose Pass 10½
Stonesty Pike 11½
COLD PIKE 10¾
CRINKLE CRAGS 12
SCAFELL PIKE 14½
BOWFELL 12½
GREAT END 14
ALLEN CRAGS 13¾
GREAT GABLE 15½
GREEN GABLE 15½
PIKE O'STICKLE 11¼
HARRISON STICKLE 10¾
THUNACAR KNOTT 11
PAVEY ARK 10¾
HIGH RAISE 11¾
ULLSCARF 12¾
HERON PIKE 8
NW
NW
GREAT RIGG 9
FAIRFIELD 9¾
DOVE CRAG 8½
RED SCREES 7¼
St. Ravens Edge 6½
CAUDALE MOOR 7¾
SOUR HOWES 3½
ILL BELL 6½
HIGH STREET 8½
SALLOWS 4
HARTER FELL 7½
KENTMERE PIKE 6½
N

HAG END to MATSON GROUND

The Route

At Hag End enter the yard and pass between the buildings, then turn left to follow a ruinous wall away. Step over it near the far end to locate a stile in the facing wall. An initially sketchy path rises over pleasant rough upland to a gateway, then skirts a marshy area before rising again, half-right to a junction of collapsed walls. Rising beyond the small depression is School Knott: the vague path descends to a kissing-gate in the far corner of our present enclosure, from where a detour to the tarn and viewpoint is easily made.

The Way resumes by turning left to an identical gate and descending a track to a T-junction. Take the track left which runs a clear, level course to the neighbourhood of Cleabarrow, becoming surfaced to join the B5284. Turn right for a hair-raising 100 yards then escape along a surfaced road to Low Cleabarrow, on the right.

As the buildings appear use a small gate on the left to descend to two adjacent kissing-gates, then climb diagonally up the field, through some trees to the next gate. Cross the next pasture to locate a further gate in the facing wall, then go straight over a quiet road and head down a field in the company of a fence between us and Matson Ground, left.

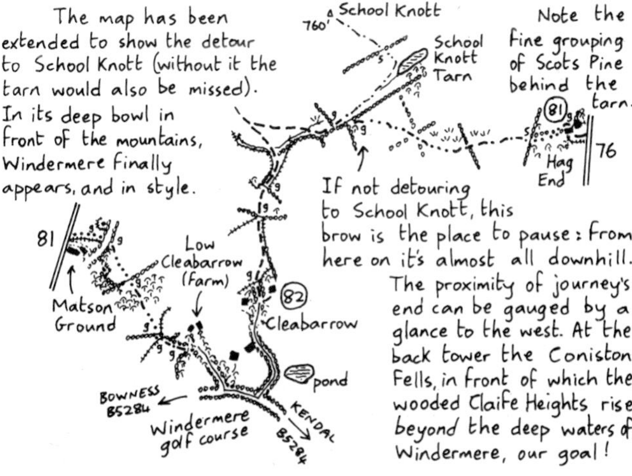

The map has been extended to show the detour to School Knott (without it the tarn would also be missed). In its deep bowl in front of the mountains, Windermere finally appears, and in style.

Note the fine grouping of Scots Pine behind the tarn.

If not detouring to School Knott, this brow is the place to pause: from here on it's almost all downhill.

The proximity of journey's end can be gauged by a glance to the west. At the back tower the Coniston Fells, in front of which the wooded Claife Heights rise beyond the deep waters of Windermere, our goal!

Bowness stands midway along the eastern shore of England's largest lake, facing its biggest island, Belle Isle, and the steep and beautifully wooded Claife Heights. The heart of Bowness is a very compact area, with its bulging gift shops a mere stones throw from the boat landings. For many visitors this is their first, and sometimes only, taste of lakeland: indeed it was the author's first, though hours of football on the grass left no time for an altar boys' trip to enjoy scenery.

St. Martins

The environs of the boat landings form a colourful scene which is best appreciated away from the height of the season, i.e. a dark midweek in February! Not surprisingly a variety of craft ply the waters, from the basic rowing boat for hire, up to the busy car ferry which shuttles unceasingly across to the opposite shore and back. A small fleet of rather classy cruisers operate a regular service to Lakeside and Waterhead at either extremity of the lake, and provide an ideal way of seeing the lake in it's true setting.

Also of interest in central Bowness are the steamboat museum and the parish church, an oasis of peace in the heart of the bustle with an outstanding east window.

The Fairfield horseshoe from the boat landings

MATSON GROUND to BOWNESS

The Route

At Matson Ground we are deposited onto the drive to Home Farm, crossing straight over and on to a third kissing-gate in quick succession, from where a path runs by some trees. Soon another such gate in the left-hand wall leaves us on another drive: go right a few yards then vacate it for a path forking left. This soon crosses a large field, turning left from the gate to a briefly-enclosed way onto a farm road.

Cross straight over and along an equally short way before following a faint track down the right side of a field. At the bottom cross a wide track between lovely woodland and continue down what transpires to be the final pasture of the Dales Way - only now does Windermere genuinely reveal itself!

At the bottom a gate admits to the terminus of Brantfell Road, which leads down to the centre of Bowness. At the church go left along the main road, purchase an ice-cream and make for a suitable gap in the boats: a symbolic end can now be enjoyed by dipping a boot into the waters of England's largest lake.

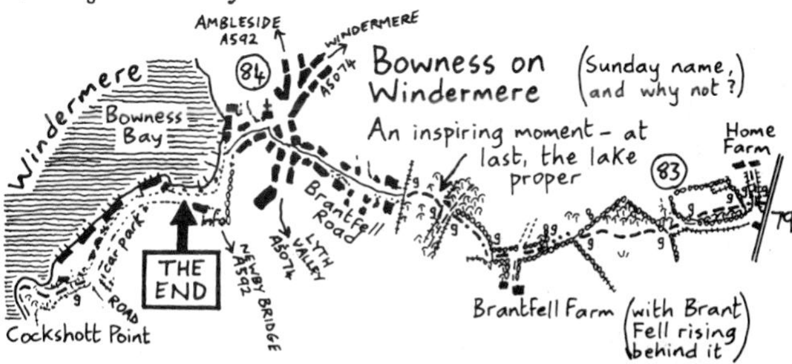

Most walkers in these parts regularly hurry past Windermere without a second glance, indeed probably showing disdain for this essential tourist halt on their way to more rugged surrounds. After spending 80-odd miles reaching it however, one can easily develop a new respect for the place. Come on, admit it, it's still beautiful.

It is traditional on occasions like this to soliloquize on the past week's events: have you found yourself, or are you grateful just to have found Windermere? Either way, continue on round to Cockshott Point to enjoy a far more rewarding conclusion.

RECORD OF INNS VISITED

Inn	Location	Comments

THE COUNTRY CODE

Respect the life and work of the countryside
Protect wildlife, plants and trees
Keep to public paths across farmland
Safeguard water supplies
Go carefully on country roads
Keep dogs under control
Guard against all risks of fire
Fasten all gates
Leave no litter - take it with you
Make no unnecessary noise
Leave livestock, crops and machinery alone
Use gates and stiles to cross fences, hedges and walls

RECORD OF ACCOMMODATION

Date	Address	Comments
3/4/03	Grassington 1st house on right next to car park	
4/4/03	The George, Hubberholme Hitch hike ⟷ Oughtershaw	
5/4/03	Low Hall Farm Mrs Oversby Near Dent	
6/4/03	Mr/Mrs Johnson Punchbowl Inn Grayrigg	

RECORD OF THE JOURNEY

Date	Place	Miles		Times		Comments
		daily	total	arrive	depart	
	Ilkley	-	-			
	Addingham	2½	2½			
	Bolton Bridge	5¼	5¼			
	Bolton Priory	6¼	6¼			
	Cavendish Pavilion	7¼	7¼			
	Barden Bridge	9¼	9¼			
	Howgill	11	11			
	Appletreewick	11¾	11¾			
	Burnsall	13½	13½			
	Linton Falls	2¾	16¼			
	Grassington	3½	17			
	Conistone Pie	7¼	20¾			
	Kettlewell	10½	24			
	Starbotton	12¾	26¼			
	Buckden	15	28½			
	Hubberholme	1	29½			
	Yockenthwaite	2¾	31¼			
	Beckermonds	5	33½			
	Oughtershaw	6	34½			
	Cam Houses	9½	38			
	Far Gearstones (B6255)	12¾	41¼			
	Dentdale Youth Hostel	16½	45			

Date	Place	Miles daily	Miles total	Times arrive	Times depart	Comments
	Cowgill	1¾	46¾			
	Lenny's Leap	4	49			
	Mill Bridge	5	50			
	Church Bridge (Dent)	6½	51½			
	Barth Bridge	7½	52½			
	Ellers	9	54			
	Rash Bridge	10½	55½			
	Millthrop	11¾	56¾			
	Millthrop Bridge (Sedbergh)	12	57			
	Brigflatts	1¾	58¾			
	Lincoln's Inn Bridge	3¾	60¾			
	Crook of Lune Bridge	7¼	64¼			
	Lowgill	7¾	64¾			
	Lambrigg Head	9	66			
	Grayrigg Foot (A685)	12	69			
	Black Moss Tarn	13½	70½			
	Burton Hill (A6)	15	72			
	Burneside	17	74			
	Bowston	1	75			
	Cowen Head	1½	75½			
	Staveley (A591)	3½	77½			
	Fell Plain	5¼	79¼			
	Cleabarrow (B5284)	8½	82½			
	Bowness Bay	10	84			

INDEX OF PLACE-NAMES ON THE ROUTE-MAPS

INDEX continued

INDEX continued